Santorini Travel - Tour Guidebook 2(

Explore Greece's Most Loved Island Like A Local. With Maps, Pictures,

By: Frosty Ezekiel

Table of Content:

Chapter 1: Exploring Top Activities in Santorini, Greece

Santorini is without a doubt one of the best destinations to visit in Greece, and for good reason. Here are the absolute finest things to do in Santorini, from calm lunches to whirlwind activities to the chance to experience some of the best views the volcanic island has to offer! Santorini is written as v in Greek.

Santorini's domed rooftops, unique architecture, and shimmering waters will be instantly recognizable to those who have long desired to visit the lovely Cycladic Island. The island is best visited over several days and is located in the midst of the Aegean Sea. It is well renowned for its historic vineyards and volcanic beaches.

What is the location of Santorini?

Santorini is an Aegean Sea Greek island. Santorini is an island in the Cyclades group of islands, so named because they create a cyclical shape. The island lies about 300 kilometers from Athens (the capital city of Greece, which is located on the mainland), 150 kilometers south of Mykonos, and 140 kilometers north of Crete.

How much time do you need in Santorini?

Aside from the world-famous sunsets and stunning architecture, Santorini has a surprising amount of exciting activities to suit every vacation style and budget.

From lounging on famed beaches to savoring local food to immersing yourself in history among centuries-old ruins, you'll need at least two to four days to scratch the surface.

One of the most important Greece travel advice I could give you is to avoid visiting too many Greek islands in one trip! It is far preferable to focus on a few tasks and execute them properly rather than working too hard and not having enough time to rest!

What makes Santorini famous?

Santorini is well-known for its stunning sunsets and lengthy volcanic beaches. As a result, the Aegean island is one of Europe's most popular tourist destinations. If you know anything about Greek mythology, you've probably heard of the lost island of Atlantis. According to local belief, Santorini is the lost Atlantis.

Is the island's real name Santorini? Isn't it Thira?

Santorini has been known as Thira from ancient times, and this is the official name of the volcanic island to this day. The island is known as Thera in Classical Greek. With that stated, if you use the name 'Santorini,' everyone will know what you're talking about, and even the Greeks refer to the island as Santorini.

When is the best time to visit Santorini?

The best time to visit Santorini depends totally on your own interests, however I would avoid going during the off season (late October to late February) because nearly everything will be closed and it would be difficult to eat out or even find a place to stay.

The ideal months to visit Santorini are probably June or September, which are immediately before or after the most popular months of the year, July and August. Visit Santorini either before or after the busiest seasons and you'll be rewarded with somewhat lower costs, beautiful weather, and less tourists.

Santorini's Top Attractions

Take in the Sunset on Santorini

Seeing the sunset at Oia is one of the most amazing things to do in all of Greece. Santorini is famous for its spectacular sunsets. Head to Oia's Caldera for some of the best views of the island, sea, and sunset.

Just keep in mind that the sunset on Santorini can get very crowded, especially during peak season (July and August), when it can be difficult to even navigate the small roads, let alone find an awesome snapshot viewpoint.

Of course, one of the best photo locations in Santorini to enjoy the golden hour is overlooking the blue domes of Oia. Other highlights in the world-famous town are the Santorini windmills and the gorgeous outdoor terrace at the Red Bicycle Restaurant, where traditional Greek cuisine is offered with a modern twist.

Admire Santorini's architecture.

Greek architecture, particularly that of the Cyclades (a series of islands named after its circular shape), is distinctive for its white-painted homes and cobbled alleys. Santorini's communities are no exception, with cave houses serving as some of the most intriguing constructions.

These homes and houses are built in volcanic rock niches and are always the perfect temperature; in the summer, they stay cool, and in the winter, the caves are easy to keep warm. Other Neo-Classical 19th-century mansion mansions erected by affluent captains may be found in practically every village and town on the island.

Pay a visit to the town of Oia.

Oia (pronounced e-ah) is one of Greece's most gorgeous towns. Oia, with its many little roads and boutiques, is possibly the most famous town on the Greek islands. The old fishing community has been inhabited for ages, dating back before Venetian domination in the Middle Ages.

Visit a winery in Santorini.

If you enjoy wine, you should consider visiting Santorini, and specifically a Santorini winery. After all, the volcanic island is home to some of the world's oldest vineyards. However, when you first look out into the countryside, you might not realize you're gazing at vines. I certainly didn't!

This is because the vines are grown close to the earth, forming a natural basket that protects the grapes as they grow. Because Santorini is notoriously windy, growing grapes along poles would result in a significant loss of crop.

Local wines are red, white, and rosé, with some of the most well-known being dry yet delicious whites!

Try some Greek cuisine.

Traditional Greek cuisine includes a variety of cold foods, sea-inspired living, and cold meat cuts. And the Cyclades Islands are no exception. Santorini is famous for its seafood, particularly calamari and cuttlefish, which are caught locally.

If, like me, you don't eat meat or fish, there are plenty of vine-wrapped leaves, olives, and tomato dishes to choose from. If you're searching for a fine dining experience on Santorini, you must go to the Red Bicycle Restaurant.

This fine dining establishment provides an open-air eating experience, and the taster menu features creative food based on traditional Greek meals. The 'cheesecake' entrée, for example, is actually savoury; the base is crumbled bruschetta, the 'cheese' portion is feta, and the ice cream is a savory tomato!

Enjoy the sun.

If you want to spend your days in the sun with little rain, you must visit Santorini! There are plenty of beaches and sunny areas to enjoy the beautiful weather, the temperature never goes below freezing, and snow is almost unheard of. If you want to visit Santorini during the greatest months for weather, go in May, September, or October!

Observe the Oia Church Domes

If you're looking for'must-see Greece,' then the domed church of Oia is a must-see. The church domes of Oia, which appear on practically every postcard promoting Greece around the world, are best seen during the golden hour. If you want the sun to set behind your image, go to the domes at sunset. Set your alarm and head to the blue domes at sunrise if you want a classic photo with fewer people!

Atlantis Books sells books.

'Atlantis Books is the most famous bookshop in Greece, if not all of Europe,' our guide said as we strolled through the winding aisles of the famous bookstore. If you go to Instagram, you'll see a lot of photos of this iconic storefront. There are rows upon rows of books to read, as well as cozy reading nooks where you can curl up with a good book.

Volcanic beaches are ideal for relaxing.

Because Santorini was produced by volcanic activity tens of thousands of years ago, the island's geographical history can be traced in the diverse rock and mineral formations found across the island. Santorini, like the lesser-known island of Milos and the gorgeous island of Mykonos, which is home to Europe's largest mineral mine, is covered in a plethora of distinctive and peculiar rock formations.

The island also has distinctive black sand beaches where you may swim in crystal clear water and rest under palm trees. Perissa and Kamari are two of Santorini's nicest (and most popular) beaches.

Both have black sand beaches with a plethora of cafés, bars, and mountains towering up above the ocean on each side of the sandy straights.

Discover Santorini's windmills.

Many of the islands in the Cyclades have taken advantage of the weather and built windmills to harness the wind power to grind flour. Santorini is no exception, with several windmills dotting the Greek island. If you're feeling extremely daring during your stay on the island, you may even stay in a windmill!

Visit Fira's Capital

Many visitors to the Greek island are unaware that the capital city of Santorini is actually Fira. The Museum of Prehistoric Thira (which displays objects from the Bronze Age) and the whitewashed Orthodox Metropolitan Cathedral are two of Fira's prominent attractions.

Take a catamaran excursion at sunset.

One of the greatest ways to see the sunset on Santorini is via boat. Consider scheduling this Santorini Catamaran Red Cruise with Meal & Drinks for the ultimate sunset experience that you'll remember for years and decades to come. This well-reviewed five-hour outing includes several beaches, beverages, and food!

Discover the archaeology of Santorini.

It's worth noting for history buffs that Santorini is home to a profusion of fascinating archeological sites. Some of the sites you can visit date back thousands of years and provide an opportunity to delve deep into history and learn about how people lived millennia ago.

Santorini's Best Accommodations

There are three primary sites to stay in Santorini, each at a somewhat different price point, so you'll want to choose your location based on your budget as well as the activities you intend to do while on the island of Santorini.

Oia

Of course, the most famous place to stay in Santorini is in the town of Oia, which is located in the northwestern part of the island and is not the capital city but is the most famous town on the island. It's worth noting that because it's the most popular, Oia is the most expensive destination to stay.

Fira

The capital city of Santorini is Fira (sometimes spelled Thera), which is located in the center of the island. It is also the principal port of Santorini and would most likely be your first point of call if arriving by boat on the Greek island.

Fira's central location makes it an ideal starting point for exploring the rest of the island. Because it is less popular than Santorini, accommodations in Fira are substantially less expensive than those in Oia.

Akrotiri

One of the more recent and popular places to stay in Santorini is a little off the beaten road but yet close to several popular island sites such as the red beach, the archeological park, and the Santorini lighthouse.

Visitors to Akrotiri will be delighted to find a profusion of upmarket and boutique hotels that are far more exclusive and private than those found in Oia. Because of the tiered nature of Oia, you should be aware that the villas are not nearly as private as you believe. You may be observed by visitors and locals while sitting in a small private pool in a hotel in Oia.

Santorini Transportation

Santorini is a big island, and if you want to view the sights away from the crowds of Oia and the hustle and bustle of Fira, you'll need to organize some type of transportation to get about to the many attractions on Santorini.

The cheapest way to get around Santorini is by bus, which is also pretty comfortable due to its air conditioning. Furthermore, it just costs a few dollars to travel between sites, making this the ideal alternative for individuals on a tight budget who want to visit Santorini.

Other possibilities include hiring a private driver, to allow you more flexibility with timings, or renting a car yourself.

However, you should be aware that the roads on Santorini can be small and steep, so you should consider twice before renting a car. Renting a quad bike is another popular alternative.

What is the best way to get to Santorini?

Although Santorini is an island, it is perhaps more accessible than you think! After all, as one of Greece's most popular tourist sites, there are numerous ferry routes that go to and from the island on a regular basis.

Finally, going to Greece is always a wonderful idea!

If you choose to visit Greece, you will not be disappointed; nevertheless, there are several factors to consider while organizing your trip, such as the best time of year to visit and other travel concerns.

Chapter 2: Santorini - Greece's Romantic Island

Santorini is known as "the island of love" around the world. Santorini, located in the Aegean Sea not far from Southern Greece, has become a popular and lovely romantic destination for couples from all over the world, thanks in part to its advantageous location, which allows for breathtaking sunsets every day of the year.

And the residents, perhaps inspired by the beautiful colors of the sky, didn't waste any opportunity to promote their home. Luxury hotels, magnificent seaside resorts, free wi-fi on the beach, intercom under the beach umbrella, and every other convenience for a memorable Greek vacation.

Every location on the beach serves as a swimming pool with a bar throughout the day, and at sunset, happy hour, live music, and a disco club are available all night. Charming cafes on the reef in the characteristic little villages pump up the volume at night and provide great appetizers paired with superb wine to be drank in front of the spectacular natural views.

Every day, the show begins again, but it is never the same: each sunset has a distinct tone, and with each excursion, there is a new flavor to discover, a new pleasant tune to listen to.

In Greece, everything is, well, Greek! Tradition is ingrained in every area, ready to enchant guests with its enchantment. But this does not happen without hard work and meticulous planning. The entire year is spent preparing for the summer season, and from June to September, the residents work tirelessly to wow the tourists and greet them with a warm and genuine grin.

During my visit, I met Ioannis, the manager of a bar on the road leading to Fira, in the heart of Santorini, and he explained how his life gets busy in May, while in winter, he travels to tourist destinations around the world to learn how other people deal with catering and reception, always eager to improve the service he provides.

The same can be said of the manager of the family-run hotel where I stayed during my vacation, who returns to Athens, his hometown, every winter to attend digital marketing and tourism workshops.

And so it went with the waitress, the restaurant owner, the gas station attendant, and the sailor who led us on our tours. The latter speaks five languages and is learning a sixth, all while planning to build a traditional Greek inn with his own hands to employ the rest of his family.

Santorini's romanticism stems from the people's love of their labor, their land, and their traditions.

Chapter 3: Compelling Reasons to Explore Santorini, Greece

There are numerous reasons why travelers come to Santorini, a Greek island known for its breathtaking sunsets, picturesque hilltop villages, and delectably fresh cuisine.

Santorini is one of the most well-known Greek islands, but it's worth following the throng to discover why. It's difficult not to be fascinated by this Cycladic superstar from the moment you see its soaring, jagged cliffs from the ferry, capped by blinding-white towns and lapped by deep-blue water that fills a gigantic, submerged volcanic crater beneath you.

It's lovely.

Santorini is a favorite honeymoon location in Europe, and for good reason. There's a lovely backdrop of whitewashed blue-domed buildings and the deep-blue Aegean Sea, and the northern village of Oia has postcard-worthy sunset vistas. There are numerous possibilities to relax on the beach, enjoy a private boat excursion, or visit a luxury spa, as well as open-air eating up on the hilltops with those breathtaking views. Pelekanos offers great seafood and spectacular caldera views. Character, a sleek Italian restaurant with award-winning wines, is another option.

It features some of the most beautiful sunsets you'll ever witness.

The sunsets in Santorini are breathtaking from any vantage point. The scene is reminiscent of a huge postcard. As the sun sets, gorgeous shifting hues of blue, red, and everything in between emerge. The town of Oia, located on the island's northern tip, is the most popular place to witness this nightly spectacle. It draws a large crowd, but the atmosphere is electrifying when the village's whitewashed homes, which are typical of the Cyclades, begin to light.

Its blue-domed churches can be visited.

Three of Santorini's blue domes are depicted on postcards. The famous trio of domes is located in Oia and belongs to two churches that are discreetly tucked away. It takes some research to replicate that famous shot, but the best place to start is in Oia's Main Square. Santorini Orthodox Metropolitan Cathedral is the most well-known blue-domed church. It is the largest church on the island and dominates the center of Fira. It was built in 1827.

It boasts lovely clifftop settlements.
Santorini is well-known for its clifftop settlements with beautiful white buildings cascading down steep slopes towards the sea. Red Beach, with its stunning red-stained cliffs and volcanic sands, is located in Akrotiri. Oia hamlet, perched high above Ammoudi's port, is famous for stunning sunsets. The capital, Fira (or Thera), is the busiest of the three and is located on the island's western tip.

Santorini boasts lovely, underappreciated white wine.
For the summer, keep Greek wine on your radar. Assyrtiko is Greece's most widely crushed white grape, and it comes from Santorini, where it accounts for 65 percent of the vineyards. The Assyrtiko grape produces dry, punchy, and high-acidic wines on this volcanic island with its ash-rich soil. SantoWines is the largest winery on the island, founded in 1947 and run as part of a local cooperative that promotes sustainable agriculture.

The cuisine is delectably delicious.
Santorini has been growing tomatoes since 1890. The fresh fruit is used to produce tomatokeftedes, a delectable local specialty of pureed tomatoes folded into dough balls and fried in oil. In general, fresh local produce is abundant, ranging from seafood to luscious tomatoes to olives. Don't leave without trying the saganaki, which is fried cheese wrapped in filo dough and drizzled with honey. Grilled seafood feasts with just a splash of lemon will be served at family-run restaurants along the seafront.

You can relax at the volcanic hot springs.
The hot springs of Santorini can be found on the tiny, uninhabited islet of Nea Kameni, which is home to the Santorini volcano. Continuous subsurface volcanic activity keeps the springs' temperature between 30 and 35 degrees Celsius - and most boat cruises will take you out here for a swim. The heated water is high in iron and manganese, giving it an orange tint that can stain garments, as well as supposed medicinal powers. It is also possible to walk up the volcano from here.

It is possible to sail around the caldera.
Book a journey out to sea on a traditional Greek caique and spend the afternoon sailing about the caldera, exploring secluded spots, hidden beaches, and even the Nea Kameni hot springs. You can even choose a catamaran with a grill or a full Greek feast with local wines. In any case, take advantage of the opportunity to swim and snorkel in the sea before drying off on the sun-kissed deck.

Chapter 4: Exploring the Historic Minoan Ruins at Akrotiri

After leaving Crete to return home, Jason and the Argonauts arrived at Anaphe and chose to spend the night there. During the night, one of the Argonauts, Euphemus, dreamed that he was having sex with one of Triton's daughters and impregnating her - keep in mind that Triton, the god of the sea, had earlier given Euphemus a clod of earth when the Argonauts were at Lake Tritonis. The nymph advised the guy in his dream to toss the clod into the sea, and it would grow into an island. When Euphemus awoke, he told Jason about his strange dream, and Jason instructed him to throw the clod into the sea. According to folklore, he followed his friend's counsel, and the clod grew into an island named Calliste; this is how Santorini came to be.

The first human presence on Santorini, according to excavations by researchers, dates back to the Neolithic Period. Around 3600 BC, Santorini was home to a significant civilization. Discoveries at Akrotiri and the well-known Red Beach showed the existence of an ancient Minoan community. The settlement resembled those found on the Greek island of Crete (such as Knossos), with various wall ornaments and pottery displaying naturalistic landscapes of animals and humans in the same ancient Minoan manner.

Santorini Island was once known as Strongili, which means "round" in Greek. Strongili was destroyed by a massive volcanic explosion approximately 1600 BC. The eruption was so powerful that many believe it was the primary cause of the demise of the magnificent Minoan civilization on the 70-nautical-mile-away island of Crete.

According to experts, the explosion was so powerful that it caused massive waves that reached the coastlines of the surrounding islands and Crete. The major landmass of Santorini collapsed as a result of the eruption, and following earthquakes destroyed much of the rest of the island. Extensive facts and studies on Santorini's volcano are now available. National Geographic has also produced a series of documentaries on the subject.

In some ancient stories, the Santorini disaster is linked to the legend of Atlantis. The Phoenicians arrived in ancient Thera in 1300 BC and stayed for five generations, according to history. The island was then occupied by the Lacedaemonians circa 1100 BC. The people of the island, then known as Thera, began employing the Phoenician alphabet around 825 BC. During the 7th and 6th century BC, Thera maintained commercial and trading contacts with the majority of Greece's islands and cities. Because of its advantageous location in the Aegean, Thera became an important commercial city and naval station throughout the Hellenistic Period.

Between 1200 and 1579 AD, the island was under Byzantine administration, and the Episkopi Gonia church was built. The island surrendered to the Venetian Marco Sanudo in 1204 AD and became part of the Duchy of the Archipelago. The island's current name was given by the Venetians after Santa Irini, a Catholic chapel. During that time, Venetians and pirates engaged in fierce fights. During Turkish administration (1579-1821), the island prospered in trading with ports in the Eastern Mediterranean. The years that followed were successful for Santorini.

Santorini's economy collapsed as a result of the twentieth-century wars, and the island's residents fled following a devastating earthquake in 1956. Santorini's tourist development began in the 1970s, and the island is now one of the world's top tourist attractions. Santorini has also been a popular destination for weddings and honeymoons throughout the years. Aside from that, many international meetings and conferences are held there in the summer, either in the Nomikos Conference Center or in elegant hotels.

Things to Know Before Visiting Santorini for the First Time

Santorini is a magnificent destination with breathtaking scenery. Every visitor who appreciates nature, adventure, and beauty should put it on their bucket list! This island's reputation for breathtaking scenery, romantic sunsets, and sandy beaches is no exaggeration.

When is the best time of year to visit Santorini?

While there is no terrible time of year to visit the stunning Santorini Island, the perfect time depends depend on your travel needs, hobbies, and preferences. Typically, travelers enjoy the most from May to October, when the weather and temperature are at their best.

If you wish to visit the island during the summer, you should plan a vacation between June and September. In these months, the weather will be hot and sunny, with July and August being the hottest. If you want to go swimming, sunbathing, and resting at the beach, keep these months in mind.

Consider going in April, May, or October if you want to have a tranquil trip when it is not crowded and the prices are affordable.

Where should I stay for the first time in Santorini?

Santorini Island is known for its wild, natural beauty, which can be found in numerous villages and sites.

The caldera edge, on the other hand, is one of the nicest spots to stay in Santorini. It is built over 330 meters above sea level and contains whitewashed cottages distributed across a 16-kilometer area that includes the amazing beauty of Oia, Fira, Firostefani, and Imerovigli. During the summer, the entire area is bathed in brilliant sun rays. The view from here is breathtaking!

How long will it take me to explore Santorini?

A five-day journey is ideal for exploring Santorini Island. You will have ample time to visit the must-see locations and have as many experiences as possible on the gorgeous island.

How to Get Around in Santorini

Getting around Santorini Island is simple and inexpensive. You can get around by hiring a car, motorcycle, or quad, as well as using a cab or a local bus.

All of these modes of transportation will get you from the airport to Fira and the rest of Santorini Island quickly and safely.

What kind of cuisine can I expect to discover in Santorini?

Santorini is a culinary destination. The meal supplied is one-of-a-kind, rich, and tasty, with exceptional flavor and reasonable costs.

Santorini offers a variety of cuisines, including Mediterranean, Italian, Chinese, and other international or ethnic cuisines that will appeal to a wide range of preferences. Nonetheless, all visitors should sample Greek cuisine, particularly local cuisine.

Santorini's food is also noted for its delectable concoctions and high-quality delicacies. You can eat your favorite foods while admiring the island's magnificent scenery and welcoming ambiance. Even late at night, there are numerous restaurants, traditional Greek taverns, and street food options.

Know what you're getting into before you go.

Santorini is a small Greek island located in the south-east of Europe. It is the most visited Greek island and one of the most popular tourist destinations in the world due to its remarkable natural beauty, which has made it famous. Before you visit Santorini, there are a few things you should know.

• Although Greek is the official language, the majority of people can hold proper conversations in English and are courteous and eager to assist. Most businesses have employees who are fluent in English and sometimes other languages, particularly in hotels where French, German, and other idioms are spoken. It is best to examine each hotel's website for this information.

• Santorini, like the rest of Greece, uses the Euro (€) as its currency. There are ATMs and banks all throughout the island where you may exchange money.

• Greece, like most European countries, utilizes the Type C electrical plug or Europlug, therefore you'll need an adaptor if you don't have one. The alternating current voltage is 220 volts.

• Remember that Greece is a right-hand-drive country. As a result, if you want to rent a car, you need get used to it and be cautious. Furthermore, if you are traveling from a non-European country, you must obtain a European driving permit.

• Santorini is a developed island with all the amenities needed for a comfortable stay. There is a hospital, health services, and private doctors, among other things.

Escape the cold: Why Santorini is the ideal December getaway

Santorini, well-known for its unique summer attractiveness, is also a charming winter vacation destination. The beautiful island, also known as Thira, is a marvel here in the south of the Greek mainland, with its magnificent volcanic scenery. While much of Europe is chilly in December, Santorini has a nice average daytime temperature of about 60°F (15°C).

So now is an excellent time to visit Santorini's quieter, more tranquil side, away from the summer crowds. It's a pleasant and friendly season here, ideal for discovering the island's beauty in a more casual setting.

In December, how cold is Santorini?

Santorini's December days are blessed with six hours of sunshine, providing ample opportunity to explore the island in a light far distant from the gloom of northern Europe's winter. However, according to holiday-weather.com, December is the wettest month in Santorini. While it may rain, the overall experience will be enjoyable.

By December, the sea temperature had dropped to roughly 18°C, which may deter all but the most ardent swimmers. During this period, the island's climate is characterized by soft onshore winds.

Minimum temperature: 11 degrees Celsius (52 degrees Fahrenheit).

The maximum temperature is 15°C (60°F).

The average temperature is 14°C (58°F).

Precipitation average: 74 mm

Six hours of daylight on average

Is it a good time to visit Santorini in December?

Visiting Santorini in December is a once-in-a-lifetime opportunity. Be prepared for a combination of gloomy, wet and sunny days. While smaller villages are quieter and have fewer open establishments, Thira, the island's hub, remains active. Oia, known for its magnificent sunsets, maintains some eateries and businesses.

The Benefits of Visiting in December

The calm of December provides a dramatic contrast to the hectic pace of the summer months. The island's stunning sunrises and sunsets can be enjoyed in peace without crowds or cruise ships.

The following are some of the advantages of visiting in December:

- Flights, lodging, and souvenirs are all significantly cheaper.
- A more relaxed attitude allows for more meaningful contact with the friendly locals on the island.
- Cooler temperatures make activities like strolling through picturesque roads or appreciating vistas from the Caldera rim more enjoyable.
- December in Santorini, as promised, offers a tranquil and cost-effective alternative to the bustling summer season, with its own distinct charm and appeal.

The Drawbacks of Visiting Santorini in December

While Santorini retains its allure in December, there are a few negatives to be aware of:

- Many restaurants and shops close for the winter, especially those outside of Thira.
- Because the distinctive bougainvillea and vivid geraniums are not in flower, the island loses some of its vibrant summer charm.
- It may be too cold for sunbathing or swimming for beachgoers.
- Some boat cruises and other summer-themed activities are not available in the winter.

What to Wear in December in Santorini

Layering is the key to comfort in Santorini in December:

- A warm, windproof, and rainproof jacket is required.
- Layer with sweatshirts and jumpers of varied thicknesses, as well as long-sleeved tees.
- Thermal vests are a wonderful idea for those who are sensitive to cold.
- Choose comfortable, heavier trousers, such as denim, as well as socks and robust walking shoes. Include hiking boots if you intend to do a lot of walking.
- Bring comfortable pajamas because nights in accommodations can be chilly.
- Remember to bring sunglasses, a sun hat, and sunscreen for sun protection.
- In the evenings, a pashmina or thick shawl is ideal for extra warmth.
- Greece's Santorini Island

Santorini Events in December

In the Greek Orthodox calendar, December is honored by numerous Saints' Days, which add to the cultural experience:

- December 6: Saint Nikolaos' Feast Day, including festivities at the Monastery of Ayios Nikolaos.
- Ayia Anne celebrated her birthday on December 9th at Vothonos.
- Ayios Spyridon is commemorated on December 12 in Oia, Pyrgos, and Emporio.
- Ayios Efstratios is celebrated on December 13 in Vourvoulos.
- On December 15, Kontohori celebrated Ayios Eleftherios.

Take a Christmas Tour

After all, it is December, and you must have a Greek island Christmas. A two-hour Christmas tour provides a pleasant way to experience Santorini at this time of year:

This tour begins at Thira's Theotokopoulos Main Square, which is festooned with thousands of lights, and concludes with a festive drink in a café overlooking the Caldera, capturing the island's distinct Christmas vibe.

Santorini's Best Indoor Attractions

1. Thira Town (Thera/Fira) Exploration

The milder weather in Santorini is an invitation to visit Thira, commonly referred to as Greece's most beautiful town. Thira, perched on the rim of the Caldera, has classic Cycladic architecture, with cube-shaped dwellings and blue-domed churches clinging to the cliffs. Its twisty, tiny streets are best explored on foot.

Thira has interesting museums for rainy days, such as the Archaeological Museum of Thira and the Museum of Prehistoric Thira. The intriguing Koutsoyannopoulos Wine Museum is located just outside of town.

A trek down the Caldera to Skala Thira port is enjoyable on sunny days. The steep slope is zigzagged by over 600 small stairs. Donkey rides and a cable car are offered for those who prefer a less arduous descent. The harbor serves as a starting point for boat cruises around the Caldera.

2. Understanding the Wines of Santorini

The inclement weather on Santorini is the ideal excuse to visit the island's famed wineries. The island is well-known for its excellent white wines, particularly those made from the grapes Aidini, Assyrtiko, and Athiri. Red wine connoisseurs will enjoy Mandilaria and Mavrotragano wineries' offerings. The most well-known winery on the island is Santo Wines, located near the village of Pyrgos.

3. Creating Volcanic Rock Sculpture

Take advantage of this once-in-a-lifetime opportunity to sculpt volcanic rock or pumice stone under the supervision of a local sculptor. This artistic endeavor is matched with the opportunity to sample local wines and food, creating a calm and delightful experience.

4. Taking a Greek Cooking Class

Participate in a fun three-hour Greek cooking session presented by Anna in her house. You will be able to create a regular family lunch utilizing fresh farm vegetables during this interactive event. Anna's recipes are not only delicious but also easy to duplicate at home. The culinary trip is further enhanced with an introduction to Santorini's wines.

5. Hiking Tour of the Caldera

The climb along the Caldera's rim from Thira to Oia is one of the most stunning experiences in Santorini. This 9.5-kilometer dirt trail offers breathtaking views and takes between 3 and 5 hours to finish, so carry lots of water. For the return journey from Oia to Thira, busses are available.

The climb begins along the upper edge of the caldera, with breathtaking vistas. The historic Skaros Rock, which was the location of a 15th-century castle, is a must-see. Oia, noted for its lovely tavernas, is a great place to unwind with a dinner. Arriving in Oia around sunset provides a beautiful finish to the hike, as the community is noted for its breathtaking sunset vistas.

6. View the Insta-worthy Sunset

For those who would rather simply enjoy Oia's sunset, there are guided walks that will take you to the greatest sites on the island for an instagrammable sunset experience.

7. Take a Cruise

A beautiful day is ideal for a boat ride across the Caldera to the volcano's rim, where a short hike awaits. Some itineraries also include a visit to the Nea Kameni sulphur springs, which are famed for their peculiar odor and allegedly helpful mud. These excursions provide the opportunity to bathe in the warm spring waters. There are several alternatives, all of which depart from the harbor at the Caldera's base.

8. Discover Akrotiri, the Minoan City.

The large archaeological site of Akrotiri, one of the Greek Islands' most notable ancient sites, is located on the southwest coast of Santorini. This well-preserved Minoan city features a sophisticated drainage system as well as interesting ceramics, frescoes, and other artifacts. A normal visit lasts roughly two hours.

9. Riding on Horseback on the Beach

In December, the weather in Santorini often feels more like Australia than Europe! Horseback riding may not be the first thing that springs to mind when thinking of the season, but it is immensely pleasurable and generates lasting memories. There are several horseback riding trips offered, including one designed specifically for experienced riders. This excursion is limited to six people and lasts two hours and thirty minutes.

The voyage begins in Megalochori, where the horses are saddled, and ends in Eros Beach. Riding along the shoreline allows riders to canter and gallop. The ride then ascends to a cliffside with panoramic views before ending with an exciting gallop on the beach. Helmets and saddlebags are provided, and there are numerous photo opportunities along the route.

Santorini Travel Tips for December

December is a wonderful time to visit Santorini because it is less crowded and less crowded. The weather is often favorable, though chilly, which makes exploration more pleasurable. However, be prepared for some weather volatility and have a 'Plan B' for wet days. While some shops are closed for the winter and smaller communities are quieter, Thira is alive with Christmas decorations and companies up for business.

Chapter 5: Streamlined Guide to Organizing a Santorini Trip (2024)

This Cyclades Island, with its white-washed buildings, blue-domed churches, and magnificent sunsets, is at the top of many people's bucket lists.

Santorini is a popular tourist destination noted for its quaint towns, luxurious hotels with infinity pools, gorgeous villages, and stunning sunsets. It's no surprise that over 2 million people visit here each year!

So you've never been to Santorini before and aren't sure where to start?

I recall stepping off the ferry in June 2015 and seeing the white-domed buildings dispersed around the caldera for the first time. It was like staring up at a postcard I'd seen several times before, but this time it was real!

Since then, I've returned multiple times and produced hundreds of valuable travel and lodging recommendations to assist visitors planning a trip to Santorini.

So, let's get started with our 9-step beginner's guide to assist you manage your Greek experience. Here, I'll go over the best ways to get to the island by plane or ferry, the best times to visit, must-do activities, and where to stay.

If you're planning a trip to Santorini soon, you'll want to make it memorable!

I've put together a nine-step guide to arranging your trip to this beautiful island. So, by the ninth stage, you'll have everything you need to have a once-in-a-lifetime vacation!

Step 1: Determine When Is the Best Time to Visit Santorini

Before choosing on the best time to visit Santorini, you need be familiar with its weather and seasons.

Santorini, as you'd expect from a world-famous island, can get very crowded.

This is especially true during the months of July and August. However, the shoulder seasons (April to early June and September to November) are the finest times to visit Santorini. The weather is still mild during these months, the sea temperatures are excellent, and there are fewer tourists.

Before determining when to visit Greece, think about what you want to receive out of your trip. Depending on your sort of vacation, the following are the best times to visit Santorini:

Budget: While many people perceive Santorini to be one of the more expensive Cyclades Islands, this is not always the case! If you're on a tight budget, visit during the shoulder or winter seasons. Due to the decreased number of tourists from October to April, airlines, hotels, and tour organizations offer lower costs.

Nightlife and festivals: The best time to visit is from June to September if your main goal is to enjoy its famous nightlife and festivals. Because these are high season months, the entire island is alive with music from bars and festivals. The Ifestia Festival (August), Megaro Gyzi Festival (August), and the International Music Festival (September) are among the top festivals to attend in Santorini.

If you're a photographer looking to capture the splendor of Santorini's famous sunsets without crowds, early November is the perfect time to come. The skies are brighter and there are fewer tourists around this time, so you can get the perfect shot!

July and August are the hottest months in Santorini. I've been to Santorini twice in the last five years, and June is unusually hot.

The winter, on the other hand, is much cooler than the summer. Although there is no rainy season in Santorini, rain can be expected from mid-October to mid-April. January and February are the coldest months of the year.

Due to the decrease in tourists during the winter months, many hotels, restaurants, and tour operators close their doors.

Top Tip: During my excursions to Santorini, I've discovered that the majority of the best settings for photography in Santorini are located outside of the main tourist regions of Fira and Oia. Gabi from Chasing the Donkey recommends Akrotiri Lighthouse for a spectacular sunset.

Step 2: Decide where to go in Santorini.

The next stage is to decide where to go in Santorini. Remember that this island is only 76 square kilometers (29 square miles), so you can explore no matter where you stay!

In Step 6, I'll go over how to find somewhere to stay in greater detail. However, here is a summary of the areas you may visit in Santorini.

Santorini tourist attractions

Oia

If you've seen images of the sunset in Santorini, they're most likely from Oia. This gorgeous white-domed town is the most popular place in Greece to view the sunset. Thousands of tourists throng to the streets and their hotel infinity pools each evening to see the famed sunset.

Watching the sunset, seeing Oia Castle, and visiting Ammoudi Bay (where I ate the most wonderful grilled octopus) are among the best things to do in Oia. During your stay in Oia, you can visit a variety of stores, bars, and restaurants.

Imerovigli

If you want to spend a romantic and peaceful vacation in Santorini, Imerovigli is the finest place to stay. Imerovigli, often known as "the balcony to the Aegean," is located 300 meters above sea level and offers breathtaking views of the Caldera and the Aegean Sea.

Hiking Skaros Rock, strolling the way to Fira, and visiting the many churches are among the greatest things to do in this village.

Fira

Fira, the center of Santorini and a great area to stay for first-timers, is located immediately across from the famed Caldera volcano. Fira is well-known for its nightlife, shopping, and colorful streets. The views of Fira will take your breath away, whether from your Fira hotel room or from the street.

Watching the sunset, traveling to the Old Port, visiting the various churches, and hiking along the Caldera are some of the greatest things to do in Fira.

Kamari

Kamari is a lovely beachfront village on Santorini's southeastern shore that is worth staying in if you want to be directly on the beach. The Santorini airport is also located in Kamari, making it an easy journey.

Kamari Beach, one of Santorini's iconic black sand beaches, is the most popular attraction. This beach has clear water and umbrellas, so you can spend the day soaking up the rays. Explore the undersea world by taking scuba diving or snorkeling classes.

Perissa

Perissa, located south of Kamari, is another alternative for a beach vacation. Perissa is well-known for its beach, which has black sand and deep blue waters. Perissa Beach, like Kamari Beach, has umbrellas, beach bars, and lifeguards.

To make the most of your time by the sea, there is also a water park, diving centers, and watersports. In the evening, you can explore a variety of tavernas, restaurants, and bars.

Akrotiri

Akrotiri is a settlement on the southwest coast of the island that isn't as well-known or developed as many of the island's other towns. It is, however, still worth a visit! Because of its location, Akrotiri offers breathtaking views of the Caldera and breathtaking sunsets.

Akrotiri features two beaches, Red Beach and White Beach, which are very distinct from the rest of the island's beaches. The main village is home to the Akrotiri Castle (one of Santorini's five fortified communities), the Akrotiri Lighthouse, restaurants, and taverns.

Perivolos

Perivolos is the place to be if you're going to Santorini with the purpose of drinking all day and partying all night.

Perivolos, located on the island's southeast coast, is home to some of the island's liveliest beach bars, with JoJo Beach Bar being a popular. Relax by one of the many swimming pools or dance the night away to the music of the DJs.

Santorini, Perivolos Beach

Top Tip: When I visited Santorini last June, I rented an ATV, which allowed me to get to spots like Skaros Rock early in the morning for shots before the crowds. Having the ATV allowed me to cram as many events into one day as possible. Always wear a helmet when driving and drive responsibly.

Not Sure Where To Go? - Think About An Organized Group Trip

Are you traveling alone or unsure where to start when it comes to organizing a trip to Santorini?

Why not join a group excursion? Group vacations are an easy way to explore Santorini because all of the preparation is done for you, with arranged activities, meals, and hotels included (varies by trip).

Another advantage of taking a group excursion is that you will be accompanied by an expert guide. Consider all of the additional knowledge and history you'll discover about Santorini.

Step 3: Determine Your Budget, Trip Duration, and Itinerary

Santorini is popular for a variety of reasons, two of which are that it is an excellent spot for relaxation due to its stunning vistas and beaches. A minimum of three days is required to experience the most of what Santorini has to offer.

I propose spending five days on the island for a vacation that combines both active and relaxation days. I spent 5 days in Santorini on my last visit, which I believed was an adequate length of time to explore the island.

Here's how to spend five days on one of Greece's most popular islands by staying in Fira:

Day 1: Spend the morning exploring Fira and the afternoon wandering the alleyways of Imerovigli.

Day 2: Spend the morning at the pool and the afternoon/evening in stunning Oia.

Day 3: Explore the black sand beaches of Kamari, Perissa, and Perivolos before watching the sunset at Akrotiri.

Day 4: Take a boat excursion to see the volcanic islands near Santorini, or go sea kayaking.

Day 5: Spend the morning wine tasting and the afternoon relaxing by the pool to watch the sunset.

Depending on your budget, here is what you may expect to spend per day (including meals, activities, and hotel) as a lone traveler in Santorini:

The budget is $80 USD.

120 USD is a good starting point.

280 USD for luxury

These are tentative budgets that will undoubtedly alter depending on the season!

Top Tip: If you're a budget traveler like me and want to save money on lunch, I recommend Gyro or Souvlaki. I found myself in a number of little Gyro shops savoring this delectable lunch, the best being 'Why Not! Souvlaki'. It's one of the cheapest lunches you'll find on Santorini.

Step 4: Think About Your Greek Visa Requirements

One of the first things you should do before making any reservations is to determine whether you require a visa.

Because of the Schengen Agreement, most visitors to Santorini will not require a visa. The Schengen Agreement permits nationals of selected nations to travel freely inside the European Union for tourism or business for 90 days without a visa under specified conditions. Australia, New Zealand, Canada, the United States, and the United Kingdom are all members of the Schengen Agreement.

If you are from a country that is not a member of the Schengen Agreement, such as China, Turkey, South Africa, Indonesia, or India, you must apply for a visa to enter Greece.

If you are from a nation that requires a tourist visa to visit Greece, it is critical that you apply well in advance and have all of the necessary documentation to ensure you can enjoy your Santorini vacation. Everything you'll need to apply for a Schengen Tourist Visa is listed below.

Step 5: Book your flights to Santorini or take the ferry there.

This is the most exciting part of arranging your trip to Santorini - it's time to book your flights!

Flying to Athens and then to Santorini is the best way to get there. The flight time from Athens to Santorini is around 50 minutes. Skyscanner is the finest website for finding low-cost, direct flights to Athens.

If you have the time, you can also take a ferry from Athens to Santorini. The trip takes about five hours on average. However, depending on the weather and the ferry company, the journey can take up to 11 hours.

If you're coming from nearby islands like Ios, Paros, or Naxos, the quickest (and generally cheapest) way to travel to Santorini is via ferry. The ferry ride from these islands takes anywhere from 30 minutes to three hours, depending on where you leave.

Skyscanner is ideal for purchasing flights, while 12Go is ideal for scheduling your ferry to Santorini.

Top Tip: On my most recent trip to Santorini, I boarded the ferry from Mykonos, which took 3 hours owing to heavy Aegean winds. Pack snacks to save money because aboard cafes are rather costly. It's also worth the trip to the top deck for some fresh air and to take in the breathtaking vistas.

Step 6: Plan and Book Your Santorini Accommodation

Santorini is one of Greece's most popular islands. As a result, there is a variety of lodging options to accommodate any traveler.

The following are the types of accommodations available in each village on Santorini:

Oia: There are some fantastic places to stay in Oia. If you want to have the entire Santorini experience, I recommend staying in one of the iconic cave hotels. There are also several hotels with private infinity pools and suites with breathtaking views of the Aegean Sea.

Imerovigli: Known for its outstanding Caldera vistas, Imerovigli's lodgings range from cave hotels to suites with private pools and views of the Caldera and the Aegean Sea.

Fira : As the island's capital, Fira attracts thousands of visitors each year, and accommodation options range from luxurious hotels to pleasant budget accommodations.

Kamari has something for everyone, from hotels with private pools to quiet, pleasant accommodations on the beach.

Perissa features lodgings ranging from 2 to 5 stars, depending on whether you wish to be right on the beach or farther up in the village.

Perivolos : From hotels with breathtaking views of the sea to white-washed houses surrounded by blossoming flowers, Perivolos is an excellent choice for budget and mid-range guests.

Akrotiri : From hotels with private infinity pools to adults-only resorts, Akrotiri is a small village with a plethora of lodging options.

Booking.com is an excellent location to browse for lodging options whether you want to stay in Oia, Imerovigli, or one of the smaller settlements on the island.

Step 7: Reserve Your Santorini Tours & Experiences

On the lovely island of Santorini, there is something for everyone to enjoy, from boat trips to wine tasting and watersports.

GetYourGuide and Viator are two locations to seek for some of the top tours and activities in Santorini. These two websites have amazing tours to do in Santorini at reasonable pricing.

Whether you want to explore the volcanic islands around Santorini or sample the island's exquisite wines, you'll find the perfect experience to fit your budget.

1. Cruise to Volcanic Islands with Hot Springs

Sail around the caldera of Santorini, hike the volcano (optional), and stop at other spectacular islands for swimming, touring, and relaxing in the hot springs (Thirassia).

2. Sea Kayaking, Sea Cave Exploration, and Picnic

Are you looking for an exciting tour that is well worth the arm workout? Take a look at the Santorini Sea Kayaking tour. With breathtaking vistas and a lunch to keep you fueled, this one should not be missed.

3. Wine Tasting Tour with a Guide

If you prefer sipping wine while taking in breathtaking vistas, the Wine Tasking Tour should be on your itinerary. With three wine properties to tour, you will have an unforgettable day. The best part is that you won't have to drive!

Step 8: Purchase Greek Travel Insurance

When arranging a vacation to Greece, make sure to account for unforeseen travel disasters such as accidents, cancellations, delays, and personal item loss.

HeyMondo provides peace of mind travel insurance for Greece at extremely low rates and has a superb, user-friendly app for managing claims.

I always use HeyMondo for my travels to Santorini these days since I like how simple it is to manage claims through their app on my phone.

Step 9: Pack your belongings!

It's time to start packing now that you know when to visit Santorini, where to stay, where to buy your flights, and whether or not you need a visa.

The clothes you bring to Santorini will be heavily influenced by the time of year you visit. However, because the greatest times to visit Santorini are during the shoulder seasons when the weather is still warm, you won't need to bring any jeans or heavy jackets!

Chapter 6: Visa Requirements for Traveling to Greece

Greece has long been on your bucket list, but you're not sure if you'll require a visa to visit its rugged mainland, innumerable islands, and bustling towns.

A valid passport is adequate for many travelers, but for others, a visa application must be submitted several months in advance to guarantee your admission goes smoothly.

Here's our guide to handling the requirements of your trip to Greece, whether you're traveling visa-free or need to fill out paperwork to obtain one. That way, you may be organized before embarking on your great Greek getaway, just as you've always imagined.

Greece visa-free travel

Greece is a member of the EU and Europe's border-free Schengen Zone, which allows individuals to travel visa-free between member nations. Citizens of EU nations that are not zone members, as well as EEA countries, do not need a visa to travel within the bloc.

Furthermore, nationals of over 60 countries can visit Greece visa-free for a total of 90 days within a 180-day period. These countries include the United States, the United Kingdom, Canada, Australia, New Zealand, Japan, and Singapore, as well as a few South American countries. To begin, make sure your passport is valid for at least three months after your travel date. You may be required to present documents stating the purpose of your visit as well as confirmation of your departure date. Check the website of the Greek Ministry of Foreign Affairs to determine if your nation is eligible for visa-free travel.

Keep in mind that you have a maximum of 90 days to travel within Schengen Zone nations. That is, if you intend to visit Italy or France, you must calculate the number of days you will spend in each country and add them together.

There is no requirement to stay in the Schengen area for 90 days in a row; you can come and go as you like for a maximum of 90 days within the 180-day period. With internet calculators developed for this purpose, calculating the length of your Schengen-wide stay is simple. However, if you stay for more than 90 days, authorities in Greece or other Schengen area nations may deport you or bar you from reentering the bloc.

Meanwhile, the EU plans to launch its ETIAS visa waiver program in 2024. If you have a non-EU passport, you must apply online for pre-authorization, similar to the ESTA process in the United States. With a cost of around €7, the procedure should be quick and painless.

Obtaining a visa to visit Greece

If you have a passport from another country, you must apply for a Schengen tourist visa for a maximum of 90 days in any 180-day period to visit Greece and other Schengen area countries. China, Indonesia, South Africa, Kenya, and Lebanon are among the non-EU nations and entities whose nationals require this visa.

Apply for a visa at the nearest Greek consulate in your home country up to six months before your planned visit. You will almost always be needed to appear in person. You must give a current passport-sized photograph as well as proof of medical insurance for the duration of your trip. You may also be required to show proof of lodging and means of support during your visit, among other documents. Your passport must be valid for at least three months after your scheduled travel date. Schengen visas cost €80 for applicants over the age of 12, €40 for minors aged 6 to 12, and there is no price for youngsters under the age of 6. Tourist visas are generally valid for six months and can only be extended in extreme situations.

If your nation lacks Greek consular representation, see this list on the ministry's website to learn which Schengen area countries accept visa applications from your home country. You may be able to apply online for visas from select countries, including India, the Philippines, and Vietnam, through Global Visa Center World. If you are a family member of an EU or EEA citizen, you may be eligible for a fast-track visa procedure. The consulate normally takes 15 calendar days to reach a decision on a visa application, but it might take up to two months. Visa extensions are rarely granted, and applications must be submitted prior to the visa's expiration date.

I travel the world as a digital nomad. Can I get a visa to stay in Greece longer?

Greece is doing everything possible to recruit digital nomads, including 12-month visas, two-year residency permits, and a 50% tax discount for up to seven years. You can apply for a long-term visa, also known as a national D-type visa, to stay in Greece for up to 12 months if you are a remote worker, freelancer, or entrepreneur from outside the EU, EEA, or Switzerland.

Apply for this visa at the Greek consulate in your home country. You must demonstrate that you are self-employed or work for a firm or organization outside of Greece. Visa holders are not permitted to work for a Greek employer and must demonstrate that they earn a minimum of €3,500 post-tax per month to meet living expenses during their stay. After the first year, they can apply for a two-year renewable digital nomad residency visa.

Chapter 7: Navigating Your Way to Santorini

Santorini is one of the world's most famous and exquisite existence islands! A small island in size, but abundant in physical products and natural beauty. It belongs in Greece's southern Aegean Sea, as one of the pictorial and attractive Cyclades islands. To reach Santorini Island, fly from Athens, Greece's capital, which is well-connected to the United States, the United Kingdom, and Canada via direct flights with many international airlines. Athens International Airport's three-letter code is ATH, while Santorini Airport's code is JTR.

Due to its amazing natural beauty and rich cultural past, Santorini is one of the world's islands whose summer holiday season typically begins in early March and ends in early November! As a result, throughout the summer, charter flights are available from a number of European cities, including Paris, London, Prague, Amsterdam, Milan, Rome, Frankfurt, and Naples. If these charter flights are unavailable on your preferred trip dates, you may have to fly to Santorini via Athens.

How to Get From Athens to Santorini

There are two ways to get to Santorini Island from Greece's capital, Athens. The first is by plane via Athens International Airport "Eleftherios Venizelos" and the second is via ferry from Piraeus Port. There are additional links between Santorini and other Greek islands, allowing you to tour the island and enjoy all of the must-see breathtaking locations!

However, the quickest and most direct option is by plane, which takes about 40 minutes and tickets can be obtained ahead of time. This method, however, is more expensive than riding the ferry. Santorini's National Airport is located in the village of Kamari, about 5 kilometers from the main town of Fira. To get to Fira Town from the airport, take a taxi or a bus that leaves from the airport station. There are other connections to other settlements from the capital.

You can take the ferryboat from the port of Piraeus in Athens, which is connected to the airport by a bus line, or the High-Speed ferry, which takes around 5 hours and is somewhat more expensive. The boats include pleasant spaces with TVs, restaurants, and cafes, as well as decks from which you may enjoy the Aegean Sea and stare at the spectacular panorama of the caldera as you approach Santorini. Athinios is Santorini's primary port, located around 10 kilometers from Fira. There is always the option of taking a bus from the dock to the capital, or you can take a taxi for a more comfortable trip. Finally, in addition to the port, there are car and motorcycle rental services.

Connectivity of Santorini to other renowned islands
You can take a ferry from Athinios (the island's major port) or Ammoudi in Oia to get between Thira and Thirassia. Stick to Athinios if you want to journey beyond Thirassia to other, more distant Greek Isles. The frequency of service varies depending on the season, but you can count on at least one trip each day in either direction. Tickets can be purchased at the ferry terminal. One-way tickets start at 5 euros ($5.59).

Because Santorini is one of Greece's most popular islands, there are numerous ferries that connect the island to other Greek islands.

Commuting between Santorini and Mykonos is possible with SeaJets' daily ferries and speedboats. Minoan Lines' daily boats from Heraklion Port make it easy to go to Santorini from Crete, and vice versa!

Blue Star Ferries operates daily ferries from Paros and Naxos to Santorini and vice versa. Furthermore, Hellenic Seaways and SeaJets provide daily ferries with high-speed boats to enable you get from Santorini to Ios.

Blue Star ferries run twice a week between Santorini and Rhodes. Visitors to Santorini are usually accommodated on the Blue Star 1 or Blue Star 2 boat. You can also take a weekly ferry from Anafi to Santorini or vice versa.

Traveling to Santorini by ferry is usually a joyful and thrilling experience. The ferries operated by SeaJets, Hellenic Seaways, and Minoan Lines are often only available during the busy season. During the low season, a Blue Star ferry sails daily from Santorini to Athens and vice versa.

While flying is the most convenient and pleasant option, direct flights from neighboring Greek islands to Santorini are not always accessible. Occasionally, direct flights from Mykonos, Rhodes, or Heraklion in Crete to Santorini are available during the summer season.

Hotel Pickup.
Getting from the airport to Fira and other places of Santorini, first and foremost, check to see if the hotel of your choice offers complimentary airport pickup. Most

hotels will most likely charge you for this service, but you should consider it because it is the most convenient and trouble-free choice for your transfer.

Taxi is the simplest and quickest way to get from the airport to Fira or any other settlement. Taxi charges vary according to season and are higher at night, between 01:00 and 05:00. Most of the time, it is less expensive than the hotel pickup, but make sure to ask the taxi driver ahead of time. Remember that during peak season, you may have to wait in a long line and share a taxi with strangers. That is why hotel pickup is still the most convenient option. Taxis are accessible outside the airport's arrivals gate 24 hours a day, seven days a week.

Bus

Taking the bus from the airport is the most cost-effective alternative at any time of year. However, there are also other aspects to consider. Santorini has an excellent local bus network, however schedules vary from season to season. throughout the hot season, there are frequent itineraries, however the bus service does not run on a regular basis throughout the winter. The bus timetable is always available outside the airport. Also, because Fira is the primary bus station, if you wish to go somewhere other than the capital, you will have to change busses there.

The KTEL transportation firm runs buses from Fira to locations throughout the main island of Thira. Most routes are served at least once per hour during the day during peak travel months, while bus schedules are known for changing frequently. Depending on your destination, ticket prices range from $2.10 to $2.81. Tickets are available for purchase on the bus. Keep in aware that KTEL buses do not run directly to locations other than Fira. To go to Oia from Kamari, you'd have to take the bus back to Fira and then another bus from Fira to Oia.

Airport Transfer

Those who do not want to take a bus or a taxi from the airport can use airport transfer services to avoid lines, delays, and problems. There are shared minivan and bus rides available, as well as individual transfers with a driver. Of course, these high-quality, dependable, and pleasant transfers are more expensive than standard ones. Make sure to locate cheap costs and book ahead of time.

By Taxi

Whatever time you arrive at Athinios Port, you will find a bus that will transport you to Fira Town in around 20 minutes. All of the buses in Santorini are air-conditioned, well-maintained, and large! If your goal is not Fira, you must first go there and then take another bus to your final destination. One hour before a ferryboat leaves Fira, buses depart for Athinios Port.

If you arrive during the day, you will find a taxi waiting for you at the ferry terminal. If your arrival is scheduled for the night, you might consider booking a ride ahead of time. Taxis will take you from the dock to Fira in around 10-15 minutes. Please keep in mind that finding a taxi to the port can be difficult. This is why most people choose to take the bus.

Although the KTEL buses are convenient, they can be packed in the summer and unreliable in the winter. If you are not staying in a densely populated city, a car may be more handy. For less-traveled routes, some people may prefer a moped (if you have a motorbike license) or an all-terrain vehicle (ATV). Rental agencies can be found both at the airport and in Fira. You must apply for an international driver's license, which you can do online through the IDL Service website.

Taxis can be found on both Thira and Thirassia. Major routes, like as those from the ferry ports to Fira, from Oia to Fira, or from the airports to specific municipalities, have fixed tariffs. Expect to pay between 10 and 20 euros ($11.19 to $22.37) for these routes, depending on your final destination. However, if you're taking a taxi across town or to a less-visited area, make sure to agree on a fee before getting into the cab. It's also a good idea to write down your final destination's address.

Transfer from the Hotel

Check to see if your hotel provides transportation from the ferry terminal to the hotel. It could be free, the same price as a cab, or somewhat more. Alternatively, you can book a dependable shuttle service with us at extremely low rates and make the most of your journey!

Using a Rental Car

You can also go around in a rented automobile. Before renting a car, take a bus, cab, or employ a hotel transfer service to Fira or Oia from the ferry port.

Using Cruise Ships

If you take a Santorini tour, you will be transported by boat to the Old Port, which is located directly beneath Fira village.

When you arrive in Santorini, you have several options for getting around the island and getting to your destination, such as using the hotel's pickup service or taking a taxi, bus, or airport transfer.

Chapter 8: Travel Routes to Reach Santorini

Santorini (Thira) International Airport (JTR)

Santorini (Thira) International Airport (JTR) is the largest in the southern Aegean Sea, located north of the hamlet of Kamari and six kilometers from the island's capital, Fira. With 2.5 million passengers traveling through each year (pre-COVID-19), it is also the country's ninth busiest airport. It has a duty-free shop, as well as a few restaurants and cafés and smaller boutiques selling snacks and pricey souvenirs.

Because Santorini is a major destination on most people's grand tour of Greece, it does get congested during peak season, which (unlike many other islands) begins in mid-May and lasts until late September.

The ferry terminal on Santorini

Ferries now arrive at the Athinios port on the island's southwestern coast. The port is at the bottom of a steep hill, and in the summer, it may become congested as passengers push to get on and off the ships. If you're first in line, you're first out the door, making it easier to beat the crowd.

If you've pre-arranged a transfer, look for someone holding a sign with your name on it, or if you don't see anyone, call out the name of your hotel.

There are also plenty of taxis and buses that will take you to Fira, Oia, and other popular destinations.

How to Get Around

Once you arrive, the good news is that, while this island is only slightly larger than Manhattan, it is still tiny enough to be easily navigated.

Vehicle rental

There are various rental vehicle companies with offices close outside the airport, including Hertz and Sixt (book ahead online in the summer to ensure a car). If you wish to travel beyond the main cities (Oia, Fira), you'll need a car, but keep in mind that traffic on the island's notoriously potholed roads is heavy in the summer, and roadways in small villages are narrow and frequently partially obstructed by double-parked automobiles.

Taxi or bus?

The bus network is good throughout the day, with multiple buses per hour to most major attractions, but after dark, the service becomes rather unpredictable. Fortunately, there are plenty of (low-cost) cabs.

Santorini buses provided by KTEL are a sleek, clean, and air-conditioned choice for reaching the island capital of Fira or heading to other parts of the island, including the spectacular Minoan remains at Akrotiri and Fira's chic cafés and shop-lined streets.

Taxis, while more expensive, are an excellent deal if you have a lot of stuff. The taxi stand at the airport is located next to the bus station (near passenger terminal one). A board displays set fares to various places, and a ticket to Fira's center costs about 15 euros. Alternatively, you can pre-book a cab.

Buggies with four wheels, bikes, and other vehicles

Hire a gourouni (pig), the Greek term for the four-wheeled buggies you'll see whizzing around the island, if you truly want to get off the main path.

Alternatively, you can do the island a favor by renting a bike in most towns, but be aware of heavy traffic during peak hours, which are from noon to 2 p.m. and from 6 p.m. onwards.

If you're an active visitor, you can also access several of the island's key sites on foot by following the cobbled walkways that circle the caldera. Just keep in mind that it may become hot here (even in the spring and autumn), so pack a hat, plenty of water, and sunscreen, and plan to hike early in the day or late in the evening.

Chapter 9: Compelling Ten Reasons to Explore Santorini

The Island is surrounded by blue water and is crammed with multi-colored cliffs, hot-headed volcanoes, and acres of sun-toasted sand. Ancient antiquities, excellent cuisine, and adrenaline-pumping activities complement nature's wonders, making your journey unforgettable.

Here's a closer look at what awaits you on the island:

1. View of the Caldera

Centuries ago, a volcanic explosion changed the island's landscape, leaving cauldron-shaped calderas in its aftermath. The island was able to endure this cataclysmic calamity by constructing infrastructure that resembled its rough nature.

Santorini's settlements are a sight to behold as they flow over the countryside. Their rugged white-washed dwellings, domed-shaped architecture, and bright decorations show themselves as a one-of-a-kind greeting party as they cling to the caldera's ruins.

2. The Spectacular Hour

Your trip to Santorini would be incomplete until you spend at least one evening in Oia to view the spectacular sunset. The village is well-known for being the best place to see the island's beautiful sunset.

As the sun sets for the day, the sky turns fifty shades of candy floss pink, lavender purple, and fiery orange.

3. Expensive Hotels

Don't be fooled by appearances. There's more to the island than just sunsets and cliffs. It also has a robust hotel business to meet your demands. It has everything you need to unwind after a long day of sightseeing, including sea-front balconies, an infinity pool, exquisite cuisine, and comfortable bedrooms.

4. Beaches with Sun

One of the world's most distinctive beaches can be found on the volcanic island. The tourist attraction is surrounded by volcanic rocks and sand, giving it a distinct aspect. So don't be surprised if you walk upon a beach covered in charcoal, white, and red-hot rocks.

Aside from that, the beach is a beautiful place to relax in the sun, plunge into the clear seas, or listen to the waves crashing into one other.

5. Volcanoes

A boat trip or catamaran ride is our favorite of all the wonderful things available here. The tour allows you to sail along the coast and visit famous spots. A tour of the dormant volcano, craters, and hot springs is included. Some visits include swimming in the calming warm waters of Nea Kameni, a location recognized for its therapeutic qualities.

The best thing is that these boat excursion packages include delectable appetizers and mouthwatering cocktails.

6. Picturesque Scenes

If you enjoy architecture, you'll enjoy walking about the island and seeing the historic neighborhoods and villages. Winding alleyways lead to intimate cave dwellings, sacred cathedrals, and neo-classical houses. They each reflect a bygone period. All you have to do is walk the streets and listen to them tell you stories from the past.

7. Historic Places

Since the first archeological investigation, the island has been associated with several historical time periods, ranging from the Bronze Age to pre-historic civilizations to the tale of Atlantis. So far, we've discovered a number of intriguing relics from these locations.

If you're interested in history, you should go to Akrotiri and view the ancient settlement for yourself. You can also visit the Museum of Prehistoric Thera or the Archaeological Museum to see the latest excavations' exhibits and spoils.

8. Delectable Cuisine from the Mediterranean

Santorini has quickly turned into a culinary attraction. The island offers everything from fusion cuisine at upscale dining establishments to traditional platters at bars. The cuisine scene is completed by fashionable gyro-joints and delectable fish.

Most menus include delightful meals made with indigenous fruits and vegetables such as white eggplants, luscious tomatoes, fava beans, and capers. The powerful

Santorinian wine and the dizzying concoction of cool cocktails provided all across the island add to the experience.

9. Exciting and enjoyable activities

Many visitors come to the island to get away from the hectic city life. They can spend hours relaxing on the beach here, taking in the breathtaking scenery. If you're looking for something daring, you can always:

- Take a thrilling jet ski ride.
- Scuba diving lessons provide a deep dive into the underwater world.
- Take a romantic horseback ride with your significant other.
- Book a picture tour to capture the island's beauty.
- Visit the enchanted castles and other historical attractions.

10. Globetrotter's Paradise

The varied travel options are maybe the most compelling reason to visit Santorini. There are numerous international and domestic flights from major Greek cities to this island. It also has an international airport 5 kilometers from the capital, Fira.

After arriving, you can take a bus, rent a car, or hitchhike your way across the beautiful island.

What if the aircraft ticket is out of your price range? Then, from Athens' Piraeus Port, take a ferry to the island.

Chapter 10: What Sets Santorini Apart as Greece's Premier Island?

There are numerous reasons why Santorini is the best Greek island and one of the world's top tourism destinations. A simple visit to the island is enough to let you recognize its uniqueness and fall in love with it. Aside from Greece's ideal environment of scorching summers and dazzling light, and the temperament of its people that captivates tourists in every part of Greece, Santorini has its own special features that set it apart and make it rightfully beloved all over the world.

To begin with, Santorini is a natural wonder of the globe. Santorini's world-famous volcano, which is a spectacular sight and attraction, built the island and gave it its current structure and geomorphology thousands of years ago during a catastrophic volcanic eruption. The magnificent outcomes of this eruption are Santorini's unusual natural beauty, the breathtaking caldera, the views, the extraordinary volcanic beaches, and the lunar landscapes.

Everything on this beautiful "canvas" is in perfect harmony. The whitewashed edifices, blue domes, candy-colored dwellings, and paved roads of Santorini merge in perfectly with the stunning surroundings, producing jaw-dropping photographs that look like picture postcards. Staying in a world-class hotel perched on the caldera cliffs with an infinity pool and a Jacuzzi will awaken your senses and make your trip a memorable one. Santorini is the ideal destination for a relaxing and romantic vacation. Remember that Oia village is famous for having the finest sunsets in the world!

Santorini's genuine core, however, lies well beneath the surface, and the true beauty lies in its people, pulse, culture, and tastes. Any opportunity to interact with locals and enjoy their warm hospitality will be extremely rewarding. What is equally satisfying is the variety of experiences and activities available on the island; sailing tours, volcano expeditions, a multitude of watersports, diving in magnificent sea beds, and hiking, or even horseback riding, in untouched nature paths will allow you extend your horizons and live unique moments. For those looking for a good time and a good time, the vibrant nightlife of Fira, Santorini's capital, will definitely match their requirements and expectations.

Santorini's archeological treasure reflects its rich history and culture. It boasts five magnificent castles worth touring, in addition to several noteworthy museums. Above all, everyone should see the archaeological sites of Akrotiri and Ancient Thera, both of which have a strong aura. This island is also famous for its delectable meals and delectable native products. Another marvel was generated by the volcanic force: a fertile volcanic area that produces tasty items with distinct flavors. The wine is, of course, at the top of this list. Santorini is well-known for its winemaking tradition, with large vineyards and superb wine varietals. Its boutique vineyards are a must-see since they provide the ultimate opulent experience.

Overall, Santorini is a popular destination because it provides something for everyone, an abundance of sights and activities, a blend of quiet and enjoyment, and breathtaking natural beauty that makes it difficult to look away. Furthermore, it is a romantic refuge like no other, with breathtaking views, picturesque places, and sunsets that leave guests speechless. Immerse yourself in its enchantment and prepare for an amazing trip!

Chapter 11: Santorini, Greece: Eight Compelling Reasons to Explore This Romantic Island

Santorini, Greece is a postcard-perfect place and one of the most romantic Greek islands to visit! This Aegean island is well-known for its gorgeous whitewashed towns, breathtaking sunsets, breathtaking views, crystal blue waters, and romantic ambiance. It's a popular honeymoon resort as well as one of Greece's most popular tourist sites. If you're considering of visiting Santorini, here are 8 reasons why you should!

1. The best sunset views are in Santorini.

For good reason, Santorini Island is famous for its magnificent sunset vistas. Santorini's whitewashed buildings standing on the cliffside, with their blue domes, are iconic. The finest sites to see the caldera views are in Oia, Imerovigli, and Fira, where there are many rooftop restaurants, cafés, and pubs with panoramic views.

Where is the finest place in Santorini to see the sunset?

There are three towns in Santorini with spectacular sunset views, but each is unique, so the ideal site to enjoy sunset in Santorini depends on your preferences. Sunsets at Oia, Fira, and Imerovigli are all spectacular. Most caldera hotels in Fira enjoy a front-row seat to the sunset over the caldera. Oia is well-known for its iconic sunset photo of the cliff, however it may get very crowded.

Aside from that, most hotels in Oia do not have a direct view of the sunset, so you must go to a sunset site to watch the sun set into the lake. In Imerovigli, I particularly enjoyed watching the sunset. It's less congested, and most hotels have a fantastic view of the sunset.

The best spot to watch the sunset in Oia, Santorini.

The sunset at Oia, Greece, is regarded as one of the most beautiful in the world. As the sun sets, it creates a golden glow over the white buildings and turquoise sea, producing a stunning view that draws visitors from all over the world. The Byzantine Castle Ruins, which overlook the caldera and provide unimpeded views of the sun dropping into the sea, are the greatest place to watch the sunset in Oia. As seen in the image below, along the walls of the Castle of Oia, that vista can get fairly crowded. This photo was taken from our private terrace suite (White Side Suites).

Similarly, the sunrise in Oia is a breathtaking sight to see, with the first rays of sunshine hitting the cliffs and sea and bathing the area in a golden tint. While it is possible to witness the sunrise from the Byzantine Castle ruins, it is less popular than the sunset because it takes waking up early in the morning. I liked the early-morning sunrise since it allowed us to avoid the crowds.

These Santorini villages offer some of the most stunning views you'll ever see, whether you're meandering through the winding streets of Oia or taking in the panoramic views from Fira.

2. Santorini is a foodie's dream.

When visiting Santorini, Greece, you will fall in love with the exquisite Greek foods and delicacies. With its rich culinary past and bountiful local resources, this foodie's paradise has something for everyone.

Santorinian specialties

Greek food is well-known for its fresh ingredients, robust flavors, and Mediterranean-style diet. Santorini is no exception, and the island's fish, fava (a famous appetizer made of chickpeas), and white eggplant dishes are among the greatest you'll ever taste. Don't pass up the opportunity to sample typical Santorini specialties like as domatokeftedes (tomato fritters), grilled octopus, Melitzanosalata, Spanakopita, Moussaka, Chloroturi, Apochti, and Fava me Koukia.

Santorini, Greece's Best Restaurants

Anogi in the lovely town of Imerovigli and Dimitris Ammoudi Taverna near Ammoudi Bay are two of my favorite top eateries in Santorini.

Anogi's menu includes traditional Greek foods including moussaka, souvlaki, and Greek salads, as well as fresh fish, grilled meats, and vegetarian options. Anogi offers a nice and appealing setting, with both indoor and outdoor sitting, and the staff is very friendly and accommodating. They are always ready to make comments and suggestions to assist you in selecting the perfect cuisine.

Dimitris Ammoudi Taverna in Ammoudi Bay in Santorini is conveniently positioned in the small fishing community of Ammoudi Bay. The restaurant is right on the ocean, with breathtaking views of the harbor and the Aegean Sea. Dimitris Ammoudi Taverna has a laid-back and relaxed ambiance with a rustic appeal that matches the fishing town setting. This restaurant is popular with both locals and visitors, and it can become crowded during peak hours. The wait, however, is well worth it for the delectable seafood, breathtaking views, and unique dining experience.

Other notable Santorini restaurants include Argo in Fira, Lauda Restaurant and Karma Restaurant in Oia, and the family-run Metaxy Mas in the traditional town of Exo Gonia.

Exploring the island's food scene is an excellent opportunity to learn about the local culture and traditions.

3. The intriguing history of Santorini

Santorini Island has a lengthy and complicated history that dates back millennia. The island was built over thousands of years by a series of cataclysmic volcanic eruptions, and the resulting terrain is both gorgeous and unusual.

Santorini was previously home to a rich Minoan culture, was ruled for centuries by the Byzantine Empire, and was invaded by the Venetians and the Ottomans. Santorini was an important part of the Greek War of Independence and is now an active volcanic zone. Today, visitors to the island can learn about its fascinating past by visiting its numerous archaeological sites, museums, and cultural icons.

A plethora of museums and cultural organizations highlight Santorini's rich history and culture throughout the caldera and surrounding cliffs. The Museum of Prehistoric Thera in Fira, for example, houses a collection of antiquities from the ancient city of Akrotiri, and the Folklore Museum in Oia provides an intriguing peek into traditional island life.

4. The Blue Dome Churches of Santorini

Whether you're interested in religious history or simply want to learn more about the local culture, visiting the Santorini churches is a great opportunity to obtain a better understanding of the island's rich background. Take the opportunity to visit some of the smaller or larger churches while in Santorini, Greece.

Most of the churches are really gorgeous, but please be a responsible traveler and refrain from climbing the cathedrals to obtain that perfect photograph.

5. Markets, arts, and high-end shopping

There are several boutique businesses, art galleries, and souvenir shops in tourist towns like Oia, Fira, and Kamari on Santorini.

Luxury Shopping

Santorini boasts various luxury apparel and accessories stores that offer designer labels from throughout the world to individuals interested in high-end fashion. Many of these stores are housed in high-end hotels or in the main shopping districts of larger cities.

Santorini's Authentic Local Markets

Visit one of Santorini's local markets or artisan fairs for a more authentic shopping experience. You can buy handcrafted items and souvenirs as well as enjoy local foods and drinks. Popular Santorini local markets include the Fira Street Market, the Oia Art Market, and the Kamari Open-Air Market.

6. Some of Greece's top wineries can be found on Santorini.

The local wine business is one of Santorini's most distinctive cultural traditions. Santorini's volcanic soil and peculiar environment create some of the world's most delectable wines.

Wineries on Greece's Santorini Island

Many Santorini vineyards offer guided tours that take you through the entire wine-making process, from grape picking to bottling. You can also sample several wines, including Assyrtiko, Santorini's characteristic white wine, as well as other varietals like Athiri, Aidani, and Vinsanto.

Popular Santorini wineries

Santo Wines, Venetsanos Winery, Gaia Wines, and Sigalas Winery are among the most popular wineries to visit in Santorini. Many of these vineyards also have on-site restaurants where you can mix local cuisine with their wines.

7. Beach life on the Greek island of Santorini

Santorini is known for its magnificent and unique landscape, but it is not always a good choice for those looking for large expanses of sandy beaches. The island does, however, have some beaches worth visiting because of their gorgeous setting, crystal-clear waters, and volcanic sand or pebbles.

Here are some of Santorini's greatest beaches:

- Red Beach is one of Santorini's most photographed beaches, thanks to its dramatic red cliffs and sand.
- Perissa Beach - Located on the island's southern coast, this long, black sandy beach is popular for swimming and sunbathing.
- Kamari Beach is another renowned black sand beach with restaurants, cafés, and shopping.
- Vlychada Beach is recognized for its unusual white volcanic rock formations and crystal blue waves, making it a quieter and less crowded option.
- Monolithos Beach is a great alternative for families, with shallow waters, a playground, and various beachfront restaurants.
- Amoudi Bay is a lovely fishing community with pure blue waves, cliff leaping, and beachside tavernas, rather than a regular beach.

- While not a beach, the Palea Kameni hot springs are worth a visit for their natural thermal waters and unique swimming experience.

8. Santorini is a Greek Romantic Getaway

For couples looking for a romantic trip, Santorini is a veritable paradise. Santorini is undoubtedly the most romantic holiday location in the world due to its breathtaking environment, lovely architecture, and excellent dining and wine scene. It's a favorite honeymoon destination because to its romantic environment. However, I would not choose Santorini as my honeymoon destination. It's too crowded for me, and I'd rather visit places in South or East Africa, such as Kenya or Tanzania.

Dining at one of Santorini's romantic restaurants while facing the awe-inspiring caldera, or watching the sun set while holding hands with your sweetheart, are unforgettable moments. For couples looking for a more private holiday, Santorini Island has plenty of isolated areas. There are various possibilities for couples searching for a romantic getaway, from secret beaches and coves to private villas with breathtaking views.

As previously said, Santorini, Greece, has some of the most spectacular views in the world, with bright turquoise waters meeting the stunning caldera. The historic architecture of the island, with its whitewashed homes, blue domes, and flowing flowers, provides the ideal setting for romantic walks and unforgettable moments. If you enjoy Greece and the Greek Islands, Santorini is a must-see!

Santorini lodging options

Oia, Imerovigli, Fira, and Firostefani are the four most popular areas to stay in Santorini. For first-time travelers, I strongly recommend Oia as a must-stay place. Oia, with its unequaled beauty, demands at least a two or three-night stay to truly appreciate its allure, in my opinion. If you plan to stay longer, I recommend spending the remaining days in a less crowded area of Santorini Island.

White Side Suites, Oia

White Side Suites is a premium hotel in Oia, a lovely village recognized for its breathtaking views and romantic environment. The hotel has stunning suites with typical Cycladic architecture, including whitewashed walls, domed ceilings, and private patios with views of the Aegean Sea and a beautiful sunset!

The suites are big and elegantly equipped, with comfy mattresses, luxury baths, and modern conveniences like air conditioning and free Wi-Fi. We had a fantastic breakfast every morning on our private balcony.

White Side Suites' position is ideal for exploring Oia and its surrounds, with the famous sunset viewpoint only a short walk away. White Side Suites' staff is also delighted to help visitors arrange excursions, shuttles, and other activities.

Imerovigli's Remezzo Villas

The elegant boutique hotel Remezzo Villas is located in the scenic town of Imerovigli, one of the most beautiful and serene areas on Santorini Island. The location of Remezzo is ideal for touring the island, with the dynamic town of Fira only a short drive away. Watching the sunset in Imerovigli is a more tranquil experience than the more popular and crowded sunset point in Oia. The Remezzo Villas provide first-rate views of the spectacular sunset.

The hotel has a variety of elegant rooms and suites that are attractively furnished and equipped with all modern facilities such as air conditioning, flat-screen TVs, and free Wi-Fi. Each room offers a private balcony or patio with stunning views of the Aegean Sea and the caldera of the island. The hotel's outdoor pool is the ideal spot to unwind and soak up the sun while admiring the breathtaking surroundings. Apart from these two recommendations, there are numerous other lovely hotels in Santorini, Greece. Booking.com has the finest hotel rates in Santorini, Greece.

Chapter 12: Categorizing Santorini Hotels by Location

To summarize, we recommend beginning your search for Santorini hotels near the caldera villages of Oia, Imerovigli, and Fira for lovely volcano and sunset views as well as a luxury experience.

HOTELS ON THE CALDERA

Santorini's cliff villages are the most popular places to stay.

In terms of lodging, they have the most options. The majority of them are luxurious and have original Cycladic architecture. The caldera hotels of Santorini provide breathtaking sea and volcanic views from their private balconies.

Oia lodging

Oia, known for its stunning sunset vistas, is not only the most attractive village on Santorini, but possibly the entire Cycladic group.

Oia gets a large number of people every day and is one of the ideal locations for your hotel because it exudes an original vibe. Its tiny alleys are lined with whitewashed cottages, blue-domed churches, and windmills, creating a postcard-like setting.

The village's location atop the caldera is ideal, providing spectacular views of the sea and the volcano.

Oia is also one of the most lively spots at any time of day, especially around twilight, when hundreds of people assemble to watch the sun set over the Aegean Sea.

While strolling through the hamlet, you will come across various little cafes, stores, and restaurants.

Imerovigli hotels

The village of Imerovigli in Santorini, built on one of the caldera's highest peaks and facing the Aegean Sea, promises amazing views of the volcanic environment.

Imerovigli is one of the most popular places to stay, offering a variety of options.

The majority of the hotels have been built on the rim of the volcanic caldera, providing a one-of-a-kind experience as well as some of the most breathtaking volcano and sunset views.

You may enjoy the native architecture and everything that makes it so unique in Imerovigli, including charming whitewashed cave cottages.

A stroll around the village will lead you to charming cafes and eateries.

Hotels in Fira, Greece's capital

The gorgeous town of Fira is the largest community and the capital of Santorini.

The streets of Fira are usually bustling with activity, and a stroll through the center will take you past a variety of tourist attractions including as shops, pubs, and restaurants.

In Fira, there are several villas with private pools, apartments, and other types, providing the chance to stay in a central location.

Several of these hotels are perched above the caldera's cliffs, providing a particularly breathtaking view of the sea and the volcano.

Regional features such as museums, churches, and galleries can be found in the village.

Fira is easily accessible by bus because it houses the principal bus terminal. You can then take the bus to any of the other places.

HOTELS ON THE BEACH

Staying on the beach is strongly advised for easy access to the beach at any moment throughout your Santorini holiday.

The volcanic beaches are unique, and finding beach hotels near one of them is well worth the effort!

Kamari Accommodation

One of Santorini's most gorgeous beaches may be found in the seaside village of Kamari.

The grey-sand beach of Kamari has both organized and unorganized areas, with various types of tourist services, including bars, cafes, and restaurants, located within a short walking distance from the coastline.

The hamlet is full of stores and other types of facilities without being overrun, making it an excellent location for your hotel.

Several possibilities are available in the region or just a few meters from the beach, in a beautiful environment where you can spend your days relaxing on the beach.

Kamari is ideal for visitors who prefer to escape the crowded villages on the caldera.

Perissa Hotels

Perissa is a little village located directly next to one of Santorini's most popular beaches.

The seemingly infinite shoreline of Perissa beach is covered of volcanic sand. The sea features clear blue waters, and the beach is well-organized, with rentable loungers and umbrellas.

Several restaurants, taverns, cafes, and pubs line the coast, just feet from the water.

If you want to be close to the beach during your visit, Perissa is the ideal location for your accommodation.

Several hotels are located in the region. Depending on your budget, many types are available, and a short walk will take you to the beach.

Perivolos hotels

You will have the opportunity to stay near one of the longest and most beautiful beaches if you choose Perivolos.

Perivolos beach is noted for its black sand, which is a result of the island's volcanic origins.

There are numerous beach hotels along the shore. The beach is mostly managed, with sun umbrellas and sun loungers for hire.

There are pleasant restaurants, pubs, bars, and water sports facilities in the vicinity, as well as resorts with rooms and studios.

The majority of them are close to the beach. Perivolos is ideal for those looking for a coastal vacation in Santorini.

SANTORINI HOTELS BY CATEGORY

On one of the world's most iconic calderas, an increasing number of hotels are springing up in Santorini. Several styles are currently accessible in Santorini, particularly for individuals who value authentic Cycladic architecture.

In Santorini, you will find hotels and accommodations for all budgets, with modern amenities and, in many cases, exquisite features.

LUXURIOUS HOTELS

Luxury hotels have become synonymous with Santorini. The island exudes a highly romantic vibe, and the great majority of units strive to provide lavish accommodations and 5-star services. Some of them also offer spa treatments.

This is one of the reasons why it is a popular honeymoon destination. Even if you are not that type of traveler, spending some additional money when visiting Santorini is highly suggested. The best way to appreciate this one-of-a-kind volcano island is to pamper yourself with endless sea views in a comfortable and soothing environment.

The majority of Santorini's luxury hotels are located in the caldera settlements (Oia, Imerovigli, and Firostefani) and are mostly tiny boutique hotels with no more than ten suites. The majority of the suites have private pools, Jacuzzi tubs, or jacuzzis, as well as patios with stunning views of the Aegean Sea and the volcano.

A luxury accommodation is projected to cost between €400 and several thousand dollars per day. It is determined by the location, scenery, services, and private amenities like swimming pools and jacuzzi spas.

The best luxury hotels are as follows:

Canaves Oia in Oia, and Grace, Chromata, and Cavo Tagoo in Imerovigli.

LUXURY AT A REASONABLE PRICE

Both caldera communities (Oia, Fira, Imerovigli, and Firostefani) and coastal settlements provide affordable luxury options.

Some luxury hotels in Santorini provide some of their rooms at more affordable rates. The reason for this is frequently due to size (they may be smaller than the other rooms), more basic and minimum amenities, or even a less privileged sea view.

There are also solutions that cater solely to guests seeking to experience a luxury lifestyle at a more affordable price. These Santorini hotels are essentially identical to luxury flats, with minor differences in private amenities, interior style, location, and services that somewhat lower the price.

The nightly rate is projected to be between €220 and €350. Finally, the season is another aspect that may influence pricing.

It's worth noting that lodging is less expensive in the off-seasons, such as spring and fall, than it is in the summer.

Best low-cost luxury hotels:

Ilioperato, Imerovigli's Xenones Filotera, and Firostefani's Agali House

SUITES FOR HONEYMOON

Santorini, with its beautiful sunsets and picturesque terrain, is one of Greece's finest romantic destinations, excellent for romantic holidays, honeymoons, anniversaries, and proposals!

The nicest honeymoon suites in Santorini are located in Imerovigli and Oia, with the majority of hotels offering them. like properties combine spectacular caldera views with first-rate amenities like as private infinity pools, hot tubs, fine dining restaurants for candlelight dinners, and other attractions in an idyllic environment.

Many alternatives also provide cave suites with a warm and minimalist style for a one-of-a-kind experience.

The bulk of the suites are lavish, but booking early enhances the likelihood of discovering more reasonable options. Early booking is essential, particularly for honeymoons. If you are traveling during peak season, bear in mind that due to strong demand, you need book at least nine months in advance in order to secure your dream home. Last but not least, make sure to notify the hotel where you will be staying during your honeymoon so they can take extra care of you!

The best honeymoon suites are:

Imerovigli's Grace and Cavo Tagoo, as well as Oia's Katikies and Canaves Oia Suites

VALUE FOR MONEY

Santorini has various options that, while not extravagant, do not fall into the category of budget accommodations. This category is distinguished by the absence of a volcano and a sea view, as well as 5-star services and first-rate private amenities.

Some of them are on the caldera but lack the uninterrupted sea views of others. The vast majority of inexpensive hotels in Santorini are located away from the tourist throng, in areas such as Pyrgos and Megalochori, or near the beaches of Kamari and Perissa. Their location is the primary component that has kept their prices reasonable. They're in great shape, with gorgeous, comfortable rooms and plenty of outside area, including a common swimming pool. The atmosphere is that of a cozy, more casual hotel seen on most Greek islands.

The nightly rate is between €120 and €220.

Hotels with the best value for money:

Casa Florina and Meli Meli in Imerovigli, Aqua Blue in Perissa, and Dream Island in Fira are also worth a visit.

VILLAS

Santorini has many villas built in various locations. Some are part of an affluent complex, while others are standalone structures.

In terms of cost, while it may be more expensive than a hotel or suite for two, it is acceptable when traveling with more than four people in a group arrangement.

Villas typically accommodate a minimum of four people. The majority of them have numerous nice bedrooms, a living area that is often divided from the dining room, a large kitchen, a swimming pool, and a terrace. They may include a tranquil garden and parking space on occasion.

They may also have amazing sea views depending on their location. Finally, because of their size, they are viewed as an appropriate holiday alternative for travelers who prefer to spend time resting at home.

DESIGN-FOCUSED

If you are a design aficionado looking for somewhere with a distinct flair to spend your holiday, this island should be on your list!

You will see some of the best examples of Cycladic architecture that blends in with the volcanic origins of the island and the Aegean sea that surrounds it. Santorini's towns are among the most remarkable architectural locations in Europe, thanks to their cubic-shaped whitewashed buildings and cave houses carved into the cliffs.

Cycladic building principles require white and basic lines, and tight restrictions protect the island's historic architecture and traditions.

On this island, you may see minimalist design at its finest. Discrete modern touches from prominent and acclaimed interior designers and architects highlight a setting's originality and transform it into a masterpiece.

The majority of Santorini's hotels conform to Cycladic architecture principles. Some are old structures that have been refurbished and converted into luxury hotels, while others were built from the ground up.

The best design hotels are:

Kamini in Pyrgos, Villa 520 in Oia, Tholos Resort in Imerovigli, and Anemolia in Megalochori are all excellent choices.

INFINITY POOLS HOTELS

Infinity pools are considered Santorini's modern hallmark architecture. They are mostly concentrated in the caldera towns of Oia, Imerovigli, and Fira.

Their distinguishing feature is that they give the impression of being on the same level as the water. This optical illusion is due to its architecture and location on the edge of a cliff overlooking the Aegean Sea. They are incredibly photogenic and help to create a relaxing ambiance.

Some have larger pools or better views than others.

Because Santorini is famous for its breathtaking sea views, it is strongly advised to reserve a hotel with an infinity pool.

Nothing beats the sensation of calm and independence that comes from swimming in a private balcony-shaped pool and drinking a great wine while the spectacular sunset unfolds in front of you like a live piece of art.

Best infinity pools in hotels:

Imerovigli has Grace, Firostefani has Homeric verses, and Fira has Cosmopolitan apartments.

RESORTS WITH PRIVATE POOLS

The island is known as one of the top luxury destinations in Greece, and it is full of hotels with superb facilities for the ultimate experience! The pools, which come in a variety of shapes and sizes and can be shared or, in many cases, private, are one of the trademark features. Infinity pools that appear to blend into the sea for a view with no boundaries, cave pools inspired by cave house architecture and the volcanic scenery, and outdoor hot tubs with views of the sea are among the most popular pool styles.

The following are the best hotels with private pools:

Imerovigli's Cavo Tagoo and Divine Cave Experience, as well as Oia's Andronis Boutique and Canaves Oia suites

CAVE POOLS HOTELS

This peculiarity has flourished in recent years and continues to attract hundreds of tourists every summer, and rightfully so.

Cave pools, a recent design trend in Santorini, are popular among honeymooners, travel bloggers, and Instagrammers.

These pools are usually found in the villages of Oia, Imerovigli, and Fira. The first section is carved into the cliff, providing the atmosphere of a cave-built-in pool, while the second is outside, overlooking the famed caldera.

It is a very photogenic and aesthetically pleasing construction that adds a refreshing and one-of-a-kind element.

Best cave pool hotels:

Sun Rocks and Dana in Firostefani, as well as Pegasus in Imerovigli.

HOTELS FOR FAMILY

Although Santorini is not considered a family destination, many couples have visited with their children to experience this volcanic island rich in history and marine activities.

The majority of hotels in Santorini are specifically created for couples and honeymooners, while others just accept adults. The number of facilities that can accommodate families in the most romantic areas, such as Oia and Imerovigli, is limited. So, if you wish to visit with your family and stay at a hotel with a world-famous caldera and sunset view, make your reservation as soon as possible.

There are more family-friendly hotels available further from the caldera and closer to the beach and the eastern section of Santorini. The rooms are more spacious, and the property has outside areas with large swimming pools.

Furthermore, the beach is close by and serves as an excellent playground for youngsters.

Finally, renting a villa is a popular alternative for family vacations on Santorini. It offers solitude and a comfortable environment in which to spend quality time with your loved ones.

Best hotels for families:

Perivolos' Santo Miramare and Kamari's Bellonias

CHEAP HOTELS

Although Santorini is not a cheap vacation in comparison to other islands, it does have some inexpensive hotels. You may have to make some sacrifices in terms of location and sea views, but you will discover wonderful spotless rooms for your stay.

The interior decorating may be dated, but if all you want is a pleasant room to sleep in and spend your time outside touring the island, an average budget hotel will suffice.

The rates range from €70 to €120 per night.

The majority of Santorini's inexpensive hotels are in Karterados, Perissa, and the area around Fira.

Best low-cost hotels:
Anna in Kamari and Costa Marina Villas in Fira
SANTORINI, ITS HOSPITALITY INDUSTRY, AND QUESTIONS
Oia is the most popular village for visitors to Santorini.

Santorini is an unbeatable choice for experiencing the spirit of Greek summer, reigning on the top destination lists globally.

It is no surprise that so many people return to recreate their summer memories, as it combines centuries-old Cycladic traditions and architecture with exquisite aesthetics and filled with a romantic ambiance.

Hotels in the Cyclades are among the most luxurious and extravagant, making it an ideal vacation for honeymooners and couples.

Santorini is known for its hospitality. That is, the quality of your stay will have a considerable impact on your overall experience of the island.

Booking the closest motel to your preferences offers a far more pleasant stay.

It is a unique location, and while we typically connect islands by open water swimming and sandy beaches, this gem gives spectacular vistas unlike any of its Cycladic brethren.

What better way to enjoy a stunning seascape than from the privacy of your own home? It's difficult to beat.

Offering a diverse range of boutique hotels, luxury suites, and villas with swimming pools in various villages and towns, you may pick between a vibrant nightlife and a calm setting for your stay.

It should be emphasized that lodging is expensive in comparison to other islands, and daily expenses can rival those of major European cities; yet, it will be money well spent.

When should I make my hotel reservation?
Because this island is a popular tourist attraction, hotel rooms fill up rapidly. It is strongly advised to book at least five months in advance. If you plan to go during the peak season, book your hotel as early as February.

Where can I make a reservation?
Greeka.com is an online travel guide to Greece and the Greek islands that has been in operation since 1999. Booking.com will conduct your reservation, or to the official hotel website, where the reservation will be handled directly. You will not be charged an additional cost in any situation.

To summarize, we recommend beginning your search for Santorini hotels near the caldera villages of Oia, Imerovigli, and Fira for lovely volcano and sunset views as well as a luxury experience.

Chapter 13: Activities and Attractions in Santorini

We've produced a list of the Best Things to Do in Santorini, which covers the volcanic island's essential must-sees and must-dos: places to visit, sights, beaches, excursions, where to dine, activities, and more.

In summary, the top places to visit are Oia town, the volcano, and Red Beach, and the top activities are boat cruises to the volcano and wine-tasting tours.

1. Take a stroll in Oia village.

Oia's traditional village is the most photographed in Greece and the Greek islands. It is the most well-known spot in Santorini for viewing the volcano and the sunset.

Oia is a particularly lovely place on the caldera, with postcard-like scenery vistas. It's a maze of cubic-shaped dwellings, whitewashed terraces, windmills, blue domes, and other fascinating structures.

What to do: Watch the sunset from Oia Kastro; photograph the Blue Dome Churches and the Windmill; eat lunch at Ammoudi Harbor; and visit the Atlantis bookstore.

2. Visit the active behemoth, the volcano.

The active volcano is responsible for the formation, destruction, and reshaping of Santorini and other Aegean islands. In fact, it wiped out the whole Minoan civilization in antiquity.

The volcano is located on "Nea Kameni," an islet facing the caldera that can only be reached by boat. Visitors have the one-of-a-kind opportunity to discover an ashen terrain that is organically ornamented with almost completely black and red lava stones. The world's largest caldera may be seen from there, as can the iconic whitewashed settlements erected on its rim.

Don't miss out on the hot springs!

Because of the volcano's high temperatures, there are hot springs where you can swim near the crater. The hot springs are located on Palea Kameni, an uninhabited islet. The water temperature can reach 35°C. The sulfur waters, which have a reddish tinge, are caused by volcanic activity.

The springs are only accessible via boat and tour. You will be able to swim in them and benefit from their healing powers.

3. View the caldera, which is a volcanic crater.

Santorini's crescent-shaped caldera encompasses the entire western side of the island.

The steep volcanic cliffs provide one of the most breathtaking views of the sea and volcano.

Oia, Fira, Imerovigli, and the other caldera communities are without a doubt the most popular destinations on the island. Many visitors come for the vistas, but mainly for the distinct atmosphere.

What to do: Some of the most exciting hiking routes in the Cyclades may be found near the caldera's edge.

4. Swim on beaches with red and black sand.

Even though Santorini is a Cycladic island, its beaches are considerably distinct from those of the other Cycladic islands.

Santorini's volcanic activity in the past created a distinct sort of beach with black and crimson sand or stones. That scenery contrasts beautifully with the sea's crystal pure azure waves!

Some of the top beaches to add to your bucket list include:

• Red Beach: This is the most beautiful beach on the island. It is named from the hue of its sand and rocks and provides an amazing sight! The beach is not well-kept.

• Perivolos Beach: Perivolos is one of the island's longest beaches, with black sand and shingle. Its waters are pristine, and the volcanic landscape is breathtaking! It is well-organized, with sunbed rentals and other visitor amenities. In fact, it is a continuation of the well-known Perissa beach.

• Kamari Beach: Like Perivolos, Kamari Beach is well-known for its distinctive volcanic environment. The beach is around 5 kilometers long and covered with dark grey sand. Sun loungers and sun umbrellas are available at beach bars, hotels, restaurants, and other facilities along the coastline.

5. Find the best locations to stay for your stay.

Santorini has some of the top hotels in the world, with spectacular cubic designs and stunning sea and volcanic views.

Grace hotel in Imerovigli, Celestia Grand in Fira, Homeric, Poems in Firostefani, and Honeymoon Petra in Imerovigli are some of the greatest hotels!

Traditional Cycladic architecture combines modern design and the finest services in Santorini to create an outstanding hotel experience.

The island's hotels are genuinely unusual, featuring cave-like constructions with whitewashed walls, arches, and other aspects of Cycladic minimalism. The infinity pool is one of the best features. Infinity pools are typically found in luxury hotels located on a hillside, such as those in Oia, Imerovigli, and Firostefani.

6. Set out on a boat tour of the island.

A boat tour around Santorini is unquestionably one of the nicest things to do.

This type of tour is very popular.

It allows you to explore the volcano, hot springs, and Thirasia island, as well as see the caldera from a different angle.

Map out your routes.

• Daily boat excursions

On a daily basis and at various times, multiple tours are offered. Afternoon sessions are ideal because you can see the sunset.

The excursion begins with a visit to the islet of Nea Kameni. You will be able to stroll on the active volcano and even reach the crater's summit. After that, you'll be escorted to Palea Kameni's islet for a swim in the hot springs. Some cruises also take you to the island of Thirasia, which is right in front of Santorini.

The fee includes pickup from your hotel and on-board food. Please keep in mind that this is the most popular destination in Santorini, so book your tour in advance!

• Catamaran cruise in luxury

Luxury boat tours on board a magnificent catamaran are also available.

The full-day cruise includes snorkeling equipment, transportation from your accommodation, plus onboard food and beverages. Furthermore, at the conclusion of the day, you will see the sunset in a unique way.

The luxury outings are only accessible in small groups, ensuring greater privacy and tranquillity.

Food is also available, with large servings and a wonderful BBQ supper. There is also an open bar.

Please keep in mind that space is limited, so book your tour early! The excursion is also available as a sunset tour or as a private tour.

7. Drive around the island on your own.

Renting a car in Santorini will save you time and allow you to visit places that are inaccessible by bus or day trip.

Having your own car will make your stay in Santorini much more convenient. You will be free to explore at your own leisure, discovering hidden and less touristic areas.

Finally, if you prefer to spend the majority of your time in a caldera hamlet, you can rent a car for a short period of time to discover specific spots you want to visit.

We offer the greatest prices and service in collaboration with the leading local vehicle rental agencies.

8. Explore the culinary scene

Santorini's ever-expanding gourmet scene has elevated the island to the ranks of Greece's best culinary attractions.

The most famous restaurants offer exquisite meals with breathtaking views of the sea.

Several taverns are also available to provide an authentic gastronomic experience.

• Traditional Tavernas

Small family-owned eateries are the epicenter of traditional Greek food. You can taste great homemade traditional Greek food at reasonable costs by visiting one.

Metaxy mas and To Psaraki, two of the top taverns on the island, are two of the best possibilities. There, you may sample genuine Greek cuisine in a traditional atmosphere.

• Fine-dining establishments

Consider dining at Selene if you want an unforgettable gourmet dining experience. It is readily comparable to the finest European restaurants, and it has embarked on a 35-year-long initiative of embracing local products and developing a distinct culinary environment.

Varoulko, Oia 1800, Lycabettus, Mr. E, and others are also good.

9. Cooking class with a local
Want to get off the beaten path and discover a more real Santorini? We welcome you to enroll in a culinary class taught by a local chef. You will have the opportunity to learn how to cook Greek cuisine, prepare your own farm-to-table meal, and partake in a wine tasting.

10. On a wine tour, you can sample local types.
The secrets to success are the weather and the volcanic soil. In fact, the island produces some of the world's finest and most known wines.

Since antiquity, wine has played a significant part in local culture and business. It is now just one of the many reasons to appreciate Santorini.

You can either explore vineyards on your own or join an organized trip.

Santo Wines, Sigalas, and Art Space are among our favorite wineries.

11. Participate in jet ski trips.
A jet ski safari, an innovative method to discover the southern coast beaches, is an unforgettable experience on Santorini.

The "south coast tour" will take you there. Some of them can only be reached by boat.

Because the jet ski safari is a popular trip, space is limited. It is strongly encouraged that you reserve yours in advance!

12. Trek from Fira to Oia.
The trek connecting Fira and Oia via Firostefani and Imerovigli towns is one of Greece's most magnificent island hiking paths. Half of the volcanic caldera is traversed by the Oia trek.

Even for unskilled hikers, this 3- to 4-hour course should be on your bucket list! It is regarded as a moderately easy hiking path with stunning vistas at every turn.

It is best to begin before dawn or before dusk to escape the scorching noon sun.

You can hike on your own, but it is best to follow a professional.

13. More caldera villages should be visited.
Don't miss some more well-known caldera communities that provide spectacular volcano and sunset views!

• Fira, Santorini's capital
Santorini's capital is the bustling village of Fira. It is an excellent location for seeing Santorini's traditional buildings perched above the caldera's high cliffs, as well as the volcano and the sea.

Furthermore, the hamlet has a variety of facilities and stores. There are numerous restaurants and bars with breathtaking views. Some nightclubs are also lively till the early morning hours.

What to do: Stroll about the hamlet, photograph the blue-domed churches, visit the Archaeological Museum and the Museum of Prehistoric Thera, eat dinner with sunset views, and sip beverages with volcano views.

While meandering around Fira, take a few steps north to the adjacent village of Firostefani. The Homeric Poem hotel, as well as its iconic installation with a caique (traditional fishing boat) on top of a terrace, is located there. Nearby is the charming "instagrammable" Galini Cafe.

• *Imerovigli, the picturesque settlement*

Imerovigli, often known as "the balcony to the Aegean," is another site to see Santorini's volcanic scenery. The area is popular with couples, especially during the golden hour. It provides the most spectacular perspective of the volcano.

What to do: Follow the path to Skaros Rock and Theoskepasti Chapel; visit Agios Ioannis Chapel; and photograph the Blue-domed Church.

14. Visit Ammoudi's little harbor.

Ammoudi is a modest fishing harbor located beneath the hill from the famous Oia settlement.

Although it is small, it is charming, with taverns serving great fresh fish and seafood.

Amoudi Bay does not have a beach, however some people swim there. After a 10-minute walk along the beach, you'll arrive to the islet of Agios Nikolaos. There will be a lot of people swimming in the waters there. The rocks provide access to the water.

Amoudi bay is also regarded a beautiful and tranquil sunset place.

15. Akrotiri, Greece's Pompeii

Visit the thousands-year-old Akrotiri Minoan ruins for an insight into Santorini's past. In actuality, the settlement is thought to have been built around 4,500 B.C.

When the volcano erupted approximately 1,650 B.C., it buried the old city.

16. Cine Kamari cinema theater.

The open-air movie in Kamari village is a popular summer activity for the entire family.

Cine Kamari has a nice garden and a bar where you can have refreshments, snacks, cocktails, local wine, and beer.

Every day, there are two screenings. The films are subtitled in Greek and are in English.

Cine Kamari has been named one of the world's top open-air cinemas. It's certainly a unique way to spend a warm night in Santorini under the stars.

Make a note of it in your itinerary!

17. Tours and transfers by helicopter

Helicopter excursions and transfers are a new trend and a popular luxury activity in Santorini.

• *Tours by Helicopter*

A helicopter tour provides breathtaking views of the caldera, volcanic island, and, of course, the volcano! Despite the fact that this new trend is not the most environmentally beneficial method to explore the island, the experience will be amazing! There are only a few left! You must make a reservation in advance.

• **_Transfers by helicopter between Mykonos and Santorini_**

You can also arrange for a private helicopter transfer from Mykonos to Santorini and experience a magnificent flight above the Aegean Sea!

Private helicopter transfers are a quick, enjoyable, and safe method to go from one island to another. They also provide an unparalleled panoramic perspective of the Cycladic environment.

You will see some of the most beautiful spots on the islands throughout your transfer. This features charming whitewashed villages, towering cliffs, and the world-famous Santorini volcano.

Unquestionably a once-in-a-lifetime opportunity!

18. Participate in alternate trips and activities.

Alternative trips are becoming increasingly popular among visitors to Santorini.

• **_Photography Excursions_**

Such trips give you the opportunity to explore one of the most gorgeous areas on the planet via the eyes of a professional photographer. Photography tours are a popular trend in Santorini, with many young people eager to participate! These tours will allow you to photograph uncommon and infrequently visited locations. Furthermore, professional photos of you with the most incredible backdrop will be shot.

• **_Kayaking on the sea_**

Sea Kayak Excursions on the southern shore are another entertaining alternative. There are two trips per day, one in the morning and one in the evening, that are suited for couples, groups of friends, and families. The tour also includes swimming and snorkeling.

• **_Tour of a Fishing Boat_**

The traditional fishing boat tour is one of the activities that is more authentic to the island's way of life.

Set out aboard a "caique" (traditional wooden fishing boat) and go fishing with local fishermen for an unforgettable supper. You will be taught various fishing tactics while your catch of the day is cooked and served for lunch or dinner. All of this while admiring the stunning sunsets and seaside vistas of Santorini.

19. Explore medieval and traditional communities.

Visit some of Santorini's traditional villages to experience the real side of the island! These lovely communities are located on Santorini's mainland and have retained their original identity by remaining off the beaten path.

• **_The medieval village of Emporio_**

Emporio, with its conspicuous medieval character, is one of the most picturesque settlements. Several restored stone mansions have been converted into boutique hotels.

As you walk through the alleys, you will notice several fascinating architectural details. The houses and monuments feature steep antique steps and modest surrounding balconies that are virtually connected. They also have arches and doors that are brightly colored. Bougainvillea trees and pergola vines offer a natural touch.

• *Pyrgos, the ancient capital*

Pyrgos, the island's former capital, should also be on your itinerary. The town is located on the mountain Profitis Ilias.

It is bordered by vineyards that yield the well-known Assyrtiko wine.

Pyrgos is a refuge from the overwhelming touristy hum of the Caldera communities, preserving the pace of indigenous island life. Its architectural components include whitewashed buildings, historic churches, and paved streets, with the castle "Kasteli" serving as a notable landmark.

Megalochori is a traditional village.

Megalochori, with its numerous paved alleyways and streets, is another hidden gem. There is a lot of local architecture on exhibit.

Megalochori is distinguished by its Neoclassical houses, azure domes, and elegant bell towers. The village also has some fantastic local bars.

20. Thirassia Island should be explored.

A day trip to Thirassia is recommended if your journey to Santorini lasts more than four days.

Thirasia is a small islet located near Santorini. It was once a part of Santorini, but it was split away due to a volcanic explosion.

It is now only inhabited by 319 people and is unaffected by mass tourism.

Santorini and Thirasia are sister islands. They share the same geology, landscapes, and views but have very different personalities. Santorini is one of the most vibrant islands, with cutting-edge tourism infrastructure. Thirassia, on the other hand, keeps a low profile by living an authentic lifestyle.

It is accessible via a local ferry that departs from the port of Ammoudiin Oia, as well as numerous organized boat trips.

21. Have some fun with different marine activities and sports.

Aside from guided trips, the island offers a variety of sports and other enjoyable activities.

• *Scuba Diver*

Scuba diving is an excellent method to see Santorini's underwater rock formations and diverse marine life!

Expect to see lava formations, lobsters, clams, spirographs, colorful sponges, barracuda, schools of fish, a little shipwreck, and other interesting things!

Also, remember to pay tribute to Jacque Yves Cousteau by visiting his underwater memorial plaque!

• *SUP*

Furthermore, Stand Up Paddling (SUP) is the newest trend in marine activities in Santorini. It's a fun way to play in the water while admiring the scenery. You can rent a SUP at Perivolos Beach or participate in an organized SUP excursion. It is a highly recommended family-friendly activity!

22. Pyrgos, the village by candlelight

Visiting Santorini during Orthodox Easter, and especially during the Epitaph walking ceremony, lets you to immerse yourself in the local culture.

Pyrgos transforms into a one-of-a-kind display thanks to the light of hundreds of candles scattered across the hamlet!

23. Art Space Gallery offers art and alcohol.

This one-of-a-kind winery and gallery in Exo Gonia combines a passion for art and wine.

One of the best things to do in Santorini is to visit the Art Space Gallery cultural hub.

While sampling wines, you will get the opportunity to view some great contemporary paintings and sculptures.

The structure was built in 1861 and is an example of the island's typical cave house architecture.

24. Views from the lighthouse

The lighthouse was built in 1892 by a French company and is one of the oldest in Greece. It is regarded as a timeless romantic area at sunrise or sunset, as well as a highly photogenic location.

The inside of the lighthouse is not accessible, but the view from there is well worth the visit. The location is free of tourists and provides a tranquil and serene vibe.

If you go at sunset, bring a bottle of local wine to taste while you sit and watch the boats pass by.

25. Do you adore animals? Pay a visit to SAWA!

SAWA is a non-profit organization created in 1992 dedicated to loving and caring for animals on Santorini.

Its sanctuary near Akrotiri is home to a slew of lovely species. Stray dogs and cats, as well as mistreated donkeys and mules, are a serious issue in Santorini. That cannot go unnoticed.

Please visit their website at www.sawasantorini.com .

More

But wait, there's more! There's plenty more to do, from fantastic coffee shops and cocktail bars to nightclubs.

We urge you to explore the island's additional alternatives, which include: • Tours • Kitesurfing • Festivals • Yoga • Massage • Spa

BEST ATTRACTIONS IN SANTORINI BY TRAVEL TYPE

With so much to see and do, Santorini is deservedly regarded as one of Greece's top tourist attractions. The island boasts a wide array of facilities appropriate for all types of guests, from couples and honeymooners to families, backpackers, groups, and solitary travelers. It is famous for its scenic settlements, stunning sea vistas, and the volcano.

Depending on the type of visitor you are, here are some suggestions for what to do in Santorini.

Best activities for couples

Santorini, being one of Greece's greatest romantic getaways, is ideal for couples. The island is well-known for its breathtaking sea and sunset vistas, making it ideal for a romantic getaway. We've compiled a list of activities for you and your spouse to try while in Santorini:

Spend the night in a cave dwelling.

Because of its snug and romantic ambiance, cave dwellings are widely suggested for couples. The majority of cave dwellings are designed to sleep two individuals. The sea views they provide are unsurpassed, allowing you to have the ultimate luxurious stay! Find the best cave houses!

Sunset over Oia Castle

Oia village allows you to witness the world's most gorgeous sunset! As the whitewashed cottages turn red during the golden hour, the ambiance of this Cycladic town becomes quite magnificent. The most well-known location for watching the sunset is the Venetian fortress of Oia.

At Kamari open-air cinema, you may watch a movie under the stars.

Cine Kamari is the island's most popular open-air cinema, and seeing a movie there on a starry summer night is a must for anybody visiting Santorini! Surrounded by lush foliage, the cinema exudes a romantic atmosphere with nostalgic touches.

Go on a wine-tasting tour.

Santorini's world-famous wine should not be missed when visiting the island! A wine-tasting tour at a local winery is the finest way to learn about the art of winemaking. You will also have the opportunity to sample various varieties of wine and possibly discover your next favorite beverage to accompany your dinners!

To tour the island, rent a quad.

Renting a quad will let you to see some of the most beautiful off-the-beaten-path areas on the island! Quads are an excellent mode of transportation for two people, especially if you want to rent something less expensive than a car. The sunny summer weather makes getting about easy and enjoyable.

Visit lovely villages.

Apart from the crowded caldera districts, Santorini has a plethora of quaint communities with a more authentic vibe where you can experience an easy-going lifestyle away from the masses. Whitewashed lanes abound in villages like as Megalochori, Emporio, and Pyrgos!

Visit the islet of Thirassia.

Thirassia, a small island near to Santorini, is an ideal day excursion for anyone looking to explore a more authentic and less popular section of the Cyclades. Thirassia has a few untouched beaches with crystal clear waters, as well as colorful traditional buildings.

Best activities for honeymooners

Santorini is without a doubt one of the world's top honeymoon destinations, with its beautiful sunsets, gourmet restaurants, and excellent lodging options. The island provides the ambiance and facilities needed to make your dream honeymoon a reality!

Stay in a five-star hotel.
Santorini is the ideal spot in Greece to hunt for luxurious accommodations! Hundreds of luxurious cave houses, villas, and suites with infinity pools, jacuzzis, and other incredible features are erected above the caldera's cliffs, providing spectacular views of the Aegean and making your ideal vacation a reality!

Take a sail to the volcano at sunset.
Santorini is famed for two things: its stunning sunsets and its towering volcano! A catamaran cruise allows you to combine everything you love about Santorini, such as a visit to the volcanic springs, Aspronissi island, and some of the greatest sunset views you've ever seen! A BBQ lunch and drinks are also included!

Riding horses from Megalochori to the Caldera cliffs
Horseback riding on the pathways of Santorini is an unforgettable experience! Starting from Megalochori, you will visit several gorgeous sites and photogenic spots while traversing the island on horseback!

Enjoy a romantic evening at a fine dining establishment.
Choose your favorite of Santorini's greatest fine-dining establishments for a romantic candlelit meal! Santorini's gastronomy scene is quite broad, ensuring an unmatched fine dining experience for all preferences. Don't forget to pair your meal with a glass of local wine! The exquisite delicacies of Oia 1800 and Selene are highly recommended.

Best activities for families with children
Santorini's quaint villages, one-of-a-kind beaches, and fascinating landscapes make it a popular family vacation as well. The island is well-developed as a tourist destination, with several family-friendly facilities easily accessible from any area. Some of the top activities to attempt for fun family time are listed below!

Visit a beach resort.
Santorini's sandy beaches and crystal-clear waters make it ideal for beachfront accommodation! This allows you to remain only a few meters from the sea, which is very helpful when vacationing with children. Perivolos, Kamari, and Perissa are the most popular beach resorts.

Participate in watersports.
Many watersports centers may be found around Santorini's beaches, particularly the more well-known and popular ones. The entire family may spice up a standard beach day by participating in interesting water activities such as jet skiing, sea kayaking, and SUP (Stand Up Paddling), among others.

Visit the legendary Atlantis 9D experience.
The Lost Atlantis museum, especially suggested for Santorini's youthful tourists, offers an exciting 9D encounter in which you will receive a first-hand view of

Santorini's volcanic explosion and the destruction of Atlantis! Visitors will learn about ancient philosophy and mythology at the same time.

Rent a car and explore the island's less-touristy areas.

Renting a family automobile is the greatest way to discover isolated locations, unspoiled beaches, and traditional villages without relying on public transportation or expensive private transfers. We provide a list of the best automobile rental companies on the island, with a wide range of vehicles available.

Visit the Minoan site of Akrotiri.

Ancient Akrotiri is Santorini's most important archeological site, with ruins of ancient settlements and other notable discoveries. It is strongly advised that you arrange a guided tour so that you may visit the site and get all of the knowledge you need to comprehend Santorini's history.

Best activities for solo travelers

If you are considering a single trip to the Greek islands, the gorgeous island of Santorini is a wonderful choice! Santorini offers a wonderfully lovely environment full with hidden gems.

Stay in Fira.

Fira, Santorini's city, is the best option for lone visitors looking for a central location. There are numerous facilities in the region, including hotels, restaurants, and stores, as well as bus stops. Its location also guarantees excellent caldera views.

Take a scuba diving course.

Explore the intriguing underwater environment by scuba diving around the volcano caldera! Scuba diving courses are the ideal method to learn more about the local marine life, the secrets of the Aegean, and the volcano's sunken portions.

Take part in a photographic tour.

Santorini, as one of Greece's most gorgeous destinations, is an excellent spot to hone your photography abilities! Grab a camera, sign up for a photography tour, and prepare to acquire the best souvenirs of your solo travel adventures!

Go on a wine tour.

Santorini's vineyards will teach you the secrets of winemaking! A wine tour is highly recommended for individuals who want to learn more about some of the world's finest wines. Participate in such an activity to learn what makes Santorinian wine so special!

Travel to different islands.

A solo island-hopping adventure is the ideal way to see more of the Aegean! Regular ferry connections allow you to visit other Cycladic islands, including but not limited to Naxos, Paros, and Schinoussa, which are only a few hours away from Santorini.

Best activities for backpackers

Backpacking in Santorini is an excellent opportunity to discover the real side of the Cyclades. The island is brimming with hiking trails, breathtaking views, and several hidden treasures. Simply choose a path and discover where it leads!

Stay in Fira.

The capital town of Fira is highly recommended for lodging because it is the most convenient location. Among other things, Fira has stores, cafés, and the principal bus terminal. When compared to other locations on the island, the settlement offers the most vibrant nightlife.

Trek from Fira to Oia.

Santorini is a perfect location for individuals who prefer exploring the island on foot, since it has some of the most impressive hiking pathways in the Cyclades. The hike from Fira to Oia is very short, but it provides amazing views of the volcano caldera and the sea along the way!

Local taverns serve traditional cuisine.

Spending a few days in Santorini is the ideal time to sample the delectable flavors of Mediterranean food! Traditional pubs on the island serve a wide range of foods created with care and using local ingredients. We highly recommend stopping at the seashore Ammoudi to sample the freshest fish on the island.

Lava-sand beaches are ideal for swimming.

The beaches of Santorini are unlike any other shoreline you've ever seen. The volcanic origins of the island have resulted in beaches covered in black or red sand and pebbles, which give a unique touch to the untamed Sanorinian scenery. Make a point of swimming on at least a few lava-sand beaches!

Travel to different islands.

If you've fallen in love with the Cyclades because of Santorini, regular boat crossings from one island to the next allow you to visit more islands in one trip. There are various types of ferries accessible, and some of the greatest nearby destinations include Milos, Ios, and Amorgos.

What are the best things to do with friends?

Although Santorini is mostly renowned as a romantic vacation, you should not pass up the chance to visit with friends! Small groups can benefit from a variety of facilities and scheduled activities, and the island's nightlife is bustling and worth experiencing! Some of the best things to do with your friends in Santorini are listed below.

Stay in Fira.

Fira is the ideal place for your stay! It is the most vibrant part of the island and, as the capital, has a wide range of accommodation alternatives. The caldera views are breathtaking, and the principal bus stop is also located there.

Take part in a jet ski safari.

Go on a jet ski safari excursion to enjoy the summer air while approaching the volcano! This excursion will take you to isolated areas along Santorini's coastline to appreciate the stunning volcanic scenery!

Helicopter flight over Santorini

A helicopter tour is one of the most popular VIP services since it provides some of the best views of the island's whitewashed buildings, volcano, and Aegean Sea. You will also have the opportunity to visit Mykonos, one of the most beautiful Cycladic islands neighboring Santorini, as part of this vacation!

Go on a wine tour.

A winery tour is a necessity for everyone interested in learning more about Santorini's wines! You'll discover how traditional wineries operate and how wine is manufactured. You will also have the opportunity to taste wines and tour the vineyards.

Take a catamaran ride around the Caldera.

Take a luxurious catamaran tour and appreciate the Aegean's cerulean waters! During the tour, you'll view the caldera settlements and the island's stunning coastline, as well as swim in the volcano's hot springs and Red and White beaches. On board, you may even order a typical BBQ lunch.

Investigate the island's nightlife.

Santorini, as one of the busiest Cycladic islands, is alive after the sun goes down. Most sites on the island have lively bars with an exciting atmosphere, and many allow you to sip your cocktail while overlooking the sea.

Travel to different islands.

Santorini is the ideal starting place for your Aegean island-hopping travels! Many additional Cycladic islands can be reached in a few hours thanks to frequent ferry crossings. You can visit as many places as you like at the same time this way!

Chapter 14: Exploring Santorini's Finest Beaches

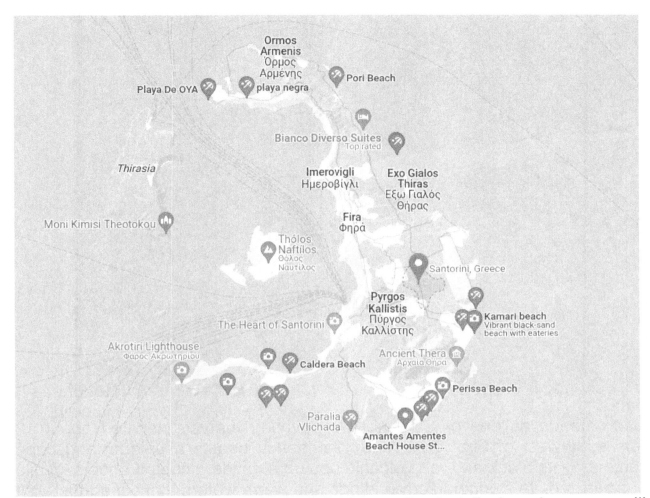

Because of their unique geological features, Santorini's beaches are unlike any other in Greece. Santorini's shoreline are littered with red and black volcanic stones, while cliffs create a stunning ambiance of unparalleled beauty.

In a nutshell, Red Beach is the most well-known beach. At the same time, Perissa Beach, Kamari Beach, and Perivolos Beach are very popular and have a lot of hotel alternatives.

It should be noted that some beaches are inaccessible by car but can be visited via a Jetski Expedition! Furthermore, due to their dark color, the black and red sand on the beaches can become quite heated.

Because Santorini is a cosmopolitan and bustling island, it can be difficult to obtain a free sunbed on the several managed beaches.

Red Beach:

Red Beach stands as one of Santorini's captivating marvels, located about 12 kilometers southwest of Fira. This renowned beach boasts a unique landscape characterized by its black and red volcanic boulders amidst pebbled shores. While partially organized, its stunning surroundings and warm waters make it a must-visit destination for those seeking natural beauty and tranquility.

The striking contrast between the crimson cliffs and the azure sea captivates visitors, offering an incredible backdrop for sunbathing or leisurely strolls along the shore. The volcanic remnants create a surreal ambiance, a testament to Santorini's geological history. Although Red Beach lacks the extensive amenities of some other beaches, its raw, untouched allure more than compensates.

Kamari Beach:

Situated approximately 8.6 kilometers southeast of Fira, Kamari Beach is a splendid resort area offering an array of activities and amenities. This well-organized beach stands as a favorite among visitors, encompassing a vibrant atmosphere and catering to various interests.

Boasting a Diving Club and Watersports facilities, Kamari Beach invites adventure seekers to explore its crystal-clear waters. Families find solace in its family-friendly environment, ensuring a relaxed and enjoyable experience for all. The sandy stretch of Kamari is complemented by the imposing Mesa Vouno rock formation, which distinguishes it from neighboring Perissa Beach.

The beachfront promenade of Kamari offers a multitude of dining options, tavernas, and cafes, perfect for unwinding after a day of beachside fun. Its close proximity to Fira makes it a convenient yet idyllic getaway for locals and tourists alike.

Perissa Beach:

Perissa, situated 11.7 kilometers southeast of Fira, stands as a prominent destination in Santorini's coastal landscape. Renowned for its well-organized and family-friendly environment, this beach boasts a diverse range of amenities and activities. Visitors are greeted by the allure of black sand, a distinctive feature of this area.

As an attractive tourist hub, Perissa Beach offers watersports facilities and a diving club, catering to enthusiasts seeking aquatic adventures. The remnants of Ancient Thera in the vicinity add a historical charm to the area, inviting exploration beyond the shoreline.

The picturesque backdrop of the Mesa Vouno rock formation adds to Perissa's allure, creating a serene environment perfect for relaxation and recreation. Its popularity peaks during the summer, drawing in a mix of tourists and locals seeking the sun-soaked shores and the vibrant beachfront scene.

Perivolos Beach:

Located 11 kilometers south of Fira, Perivolos Beach stands as a quintessential Santorini gem, known for its expansive stretch of black sand. Renowned as Santorini's longest black sand beach, Perivolos beckons travelers with its well-organized and vibrant atmosphere.

A hub for tourists, Perivolos offers an array of watersports activities along its sandy shores, inviting thrill-seekers to indulge in jet skiing, windsurfing, and more. The family-friendly environment ensures a pleasant and enjoyable visit for visitors of all ages.

The beachfront is adorned with an assortment of hotels, tavernas, and beach bars, creating a lively atmosphere. Travelers can relish in the diverse culinary delights and vibrant nightlife that Perivolos has to offer, making it a sought-after destination for both daytime relaxation and evening entertainment.

Vlychada Beach:

Nestled 10 kilometers south of Fira, Vlychada Beach is a picturesque haven on Santorini's southern coast. Embraced by dramatic cliffs and black sand, this partially organized beach boasts a charming and tranquil ambiance, attracting nature enthusiasts and beachgoers alike.

During the summer, Vlychada Beach transforms into a picturesque scene with a small harbor that welcomes fishing boats and yachts. Its serene surroundings and sandy shores offer visitors the perfect spot to unwind, sunbathe, or take leisurely walks along the coastline.

The raw beauty of Vlychada, set against a backdrop of rugged cliffs, creates an enchanting setting that captivates visitors seeking a peaceful retreat amidst Santorini's stunning natural landscapes.

Agios Georgios Beach:

Nestled 11 kilometers southeast of Fira, Agios Georgios Beach stands as a prominent destination in the southernmost region of Santorini. With its well-organized setting and picturesque surroundings, Agios Georgios Beach entices visitors with its unique charm.

This partially organized sandy beach offers a range of watersports activities, inviting enthusiasts to indulge in thrilling experiences amidst the stunning coastal backdrop. The presence of black stones scattered along the shoreline adds to its distinctive allure, setting it apart as one of Santorini's popular tourist spots.

The inviting waters and family-friendly atmosphere ensure a delightful and relaxing beach experience for visitors, whether enjoying the sunshine, partaking in aquatic adventures, or simply strolling along the tranquil shores.

Cape Columbo Beach:

Situated 8.5 kilometers northeast of Fira, Cape Columbo Beach is a secluded and unspoiled gem on Santorini's northeastern coast. This unique beach stands out for its pebbled terrain, secluded nature, and nudist-friendly atmosphere.

Amidst a rugged landscape, Cape Columbo's pebbled shores offer a sense of seclusion and tranquility. It remains an unorganized and relatively untouched area, attracting those seeking a serene and uncrowded beach experience.

The beach's remote location and natural surroundings make it a favorite among visitors desiring privacy and solitude. While the beach is not equipped with amenities, its unspoiled beauty and tranquil atmosphere appeal to those seeking a more off-the-beaten-path beach adventure.

Monolithos Beach:

Located 6 kilometers east of Fira, the Monolithos Beach stands out as a family-friendly destination in Santorini. Its pebbled, secluded, and unorganized setting offers a serene escape. The coastline is complemented by a range of hotels bordering the shore, providing convenient amenities and facilities for visitors.

This inviting beach is well-suited for families, featuring a play area and a volley court, ensuring a fun-filled day for children and adults alike. The laid-back ambiance, coupled with the picturesque coastal views, makes Monolithos a delightful retreat for families seeking both relaxation and entertainment by the sea.

White Beach:

White Beach, situated 13.4 kilometers southwest of Fira, stands as a secluded cove adjacent to the famous Red Beach. Similar to its red-hued counterpart, White Beach boasts black stones adorning its shores, contrasting against the surrounding white cliffs.

Although unorganized and secluded, White Beach is a nudist-friendly destination offering a tranquil environment for visitors seeking privacy. The striking landscape, coupled with the unique interplay of black pebbles and white cliffs, creates a serene setting, inviting beachgoers to indulge in the natural beauty of Santorini's coastline.

Vourvoulos Beach:

Approximately 4.5 kilometers northeast of Fira, Vourvoulos Beach stands as a picturesque pebbled shoreline. Despite its alluring beauty, frequent strong winds in the area can make swimming challenging, with occasional large waves.

This secluded and unorganized beach offers a serene atmosphere for relaxation, although visitors might find the waters less suitable for swimming due to the prevailing wind conditions. Nevertheless, the scenic beauty of Vourvoulos Beach remains a draw for those seeking a peaceful retreat amidst Santorini's coastal landscapes.

Baxedes Beach:

Located 10 kilometers northwest of Fira, Baxedes Beach sits in the northern section of Santorini, close to Oia. This nudist-friendly, secluded, and unorganized beach offers a remote and serene escape for beachgoers seeking privacy and tranquility.

Its remote location adds to its appeal, attracting visitors looking to explore the quieter side of Santorini's coastline. With its pebbled terrain and unspoiled ambiance, Baxedes Beach provides an ideal setting for a serene day by the sea.

Armeni Beach:

Nestled below Oia's village, Armeni Beach stands as a charming coastline made up of black and red volcanic pebbles. This unorganized, pebbled beach features a small harbor and offers visitors a glimpse into the picturesque beauty of a Mediterranean village.

Accessed by boat or via a steep stairway from Oia, Armeni Beach allures travelers with its unique character and stunning coastal vistas. Its remote and unspoiled nature provides an ideal spot for a peaceful retreat away from the bustling crowds.

Gialos Beach:

Situated 9 kilometers south of Fira, Gialos Beach offers a secluded and unorganized setting, providing visitors with breathtaking views of the Santorini volcano. Its remote location contributes to its serene ambiance, attracting those seeking a quieter beach experience.

The tranquil surroundings and unspoiled beauty of Gialos Beach make it an inviting spot to relax and soak in the natural splendor of Santorini's coastline.

Exomitis Beach:

Exomitis Beach, located 13 kilometers south of Fira, marks the termination point of Perissa's extensive black sand beach. This unorganized beach features a mix of sandy and pebbled terrain, offering a quieter alternative to its neighboring bustling spots.

Its proximity to Vlychada positions it as an extension of the coastline, allowing visitors to explore the different facets of Santorini's coastal beauty. The unpretentious charm of Exomitis Beach makes it an ideal spot for a peaceful seaside retreat away from the more crowded areas.

Kambia Beach:

Found 14 kilometers southwest of Fira, Kambia Beach is a secluded and unorganized gem nestled between the popular Red and White beaches. This tranquil coastline offers visitors a serene escape with its pebbled and unspoiled setting.

As a remote destination, Kambia Beach provides a sense of seclusion, making it an ideal spot for visitors seeking a quieter beach experience away from the more frequented areas of Santorini.

Caldera Beach:

Situated 10 kilometers southwest of Fira, Caldera Beach stands as a secluded and unorganized gem nestled north of Akrotiri. Known for its unspoiled nature and deep waters, this small beach offers visitors a wild and serene escape.

Caldera Beach's rugged beauty and remote location make it an ideal destination for those seeking an off-the-beaten-path experience amidst Santorini's stunning coastal landscapes.

Each of these beaches in Santorini offers a unique blend of natural beauty, tranquility, and distinct character, appealing to visitors seeking varied experiences along the island's captivating coastline.

Xiropigado Beach:

Located 5 kilometers northeast of Fira, Xiropigado Beach is a secluded, unorganized pebbled beach nestled between the charming beaches of Pori and Vourvoulos. Its remote setting offers visitors a tranquil escape amidst Santorini's coastal landscapes.

As an unspoiled gem, Xiropigado Beach provides a serene environment for those seeking solitude and natural beauty. With its pebbled terrain and secluded ambiance, it stands as an ideal spot for a quiet day by the sea.

Mesa Pigadia Beach:

Mesa Pigadia Beach, positioned 14 kilometers southwest of Fira, is a partially organized pebbled beach close to the village of Akrotiri. This serene shoreline offers visitors a peaceful retreat amidst its secluded and unspoiled setting.

The beach's partial organization ensures a comfortable experience for visitors while retaining its natural charm. Mesa Pigadia's pebbled terrain and tranquil atmosphere make it an inviting spot for relaxation and unwinding by the sea.

Pori Beach:

Nestled 6 kilometers north of Fira, Pori Beach stands as a tranquil and secluded spot on Santorini's east shore. Its unorganized and pebbled terrain provides an idyllic setting for leisurely beach activities.

Known for its serene ambiance, Pori Beach invites visitors to enjoy a peaceful day away from the hustle and bustle. The unspoiled nature of this coastline makes it a serene escape for beachgoers seeking tranquility.

Katharos Beach:

Situated 1 kilometer north of Oia, Katharos Beach offers a secluded and unorganized pebbled shoreline on Santorini's northwestern coast. Its remote location provides a serene setting for visitors seeking a quiet retreat.

Katharos Beach's secluded nature, complemented by its pebbled terrain, makes it an ideal spot to enjoy the peacefulness of Santorini's coastal beauty away from the crowds.

Paradise Beach:

Located 3 kilometers north of Oia, Paradise Beach stands as a secluded, unorganized pebbled shoreline, serving as a natural extension of Baxedes Beach. This tranquil coastal spot caters to individuals seeking isolated and serene seashores.

Its unspoiled nature and secluded ambiance make it an inviting spot for visitors who prefer a quieter beach experience amidst Santorini's captivating coastal landscapes.

Chapter 15: Exploring Tours and Excursions in Santorini

In summary, the most popular tours are boat journeys to the Volcano and Hot Springs, wine sampling at the numerous vineyards, and jet ski explorations.

They are available from April to October to provide unique holiday experiences. Make a reservation in advance! The tours are extremely popular.

Santorini offers visitors a wealth of interesting locations. The majestic active volcano, the charming Oia, and the unforgettable sunset are only a few examples. Tours in Santorini are the ideal way to absorb up as much knowledge and as many unique sights as possible during your visit.

SAILING AND BOATING

Boat trips are a popular way to experience Santorini's seascape; they provide the ideal opportunity to explore the Aegean's crystal blue waters while approaching the island's or volcano's interesting coastline.

Boat excursions are a peaceful pastime that typically involve snorkeling, hiking, lunch or dinner, and visits to the volcano, hot springs, or Thirassia. Some are available during the day, while others are only available in the evening for sunset viewing. Depending on the tour you choose, wine tasting, fishing, and other activities may be included.

Check out the Sunset boat tour to Volcano, Hot Springs, Thirassia & Oia, and Sunset and Dinner on Board for a memorable journey by boat to the volcano and Thirassia or the hot springs!

Day Sailing Cruise aboard a luxurious catamaran allows you to see the caldera settlements from the seaside for day sailing cruises. It also includes a swim in the hot springs and visits to several of the area's most popular beaches. The identical one is available in a nighttime form.

HISTORY

If you don't think history is for you, be prepared to alter your mind! Fortunately, history trips do not entail tedious textbooks. On the contrary, engaging family activities have taken over in Santorini!

The Akrotiri Guided Tour is the greatest method to relive the island's glorious days. It takes place at the Minoan site of Akrotiri, one of the most important Minoan settlements in the Aegean Sea. A expert guide will take you around the location of the mythical city of Atlantis.

If legend-hunting appeals to you, then the Lost Atlantis 9D Experience is for you! It is the world's first museum dedicated to the myth of Lost Atlantis, and it provides an unforgettable infotainment experience! The 9D experience will captivate both youngsters and adults due to its revolutionary innovations.

SIGHTSEEING

Whether you plan to stay for a few days or a week, we recommend arranging a tour that will introduce you to the island's attractions, environment, and cultural legacy.

A bus tour of the island takes you to various must-see destinations, including the archeological site of Akrotiri, a winery, Perivolos beach, Oia town, and others.

This type of tour allows visitors to get a taste of the nicest sections of the island while remaining comfortable.

HELICOPTER

Because getting to the sights can be difficult during peak season, helicopter tours provide a unique alternative to traditional sightseeing. A helicopter ride above the volcano and Oia allows guests to avoid the sweltering heat and crowds while admiring the spectacular scenery from above.

If you want to explore the trendy Mykonos, a helicopter transfer from one location to another is also accessible!

PRIVATE

Private tours in Santorini are highly suggested for couples and small groups of up to four individuals, allowing you to relax and explore the island at your leisure. This tour has been created to add a touch of luxury to your stay by allowing you to enjoy some of the island's best-kept secrets.

When it comes to private cruises, the Private catamaran trip with BBQ is hands away the finest option for couples wishing to explore the coastline and the volcano.

The cruise departs from Ammoudi's lovely harbor and takes you to the famed Red Beach and Mesa Pigadia for a swim in the crystal clear seas. You will also explore the hot springs and experience its medicinal effects before visiting one of Santorini's most iconic sites, the 19th-century lighthouse.

The cruise is offered in both the morning and evening. It concludes with a BBQ lunch or dinner with traditional Greek dishes paired with the finest local wines.

EXPERIENCES FROM VOLCANO VISITS

The enormous volcano, the iconic landmark that created and altered the island, should not be missed by any tourist. The greatest way to explore the magnificence of Santorini's untamed terrain is to board a boat for an exciting volcano tour!

It allows access to the active volcano and wandering along the crater rim.

The Volcano and Hot Springs Boat Tour, which combines a trip to the volcano with a visit to the hot springs at Palea Kameni islet, is one of the most worthwhile trips in Santorini. You should not pass up the opportunity to profit from the hot waters!

The Volcano, Hot Springs, and Thirassia Boat Tour, on the other hand, includes an extra stop in Thirassia. Santorini and its tranquil sister island are diametrically opposed! Thirassia's stunning attractiveness stems from its natural beauty. Thirassia, with only a few permanent residents, has avoided tourist growth, preserving its genuine character.

WINE-TASTING

Viniculture is an important part of local culture; the wines produced are well-known all over the world.

Winery visits and wine-tasting tours in Santorini are among the most popular activities to undertake if you want to learn more about winemaking and wine tasting. Wine-tasting events are available to fulfill the demands of all wine enthusiasts. Visiting different wineries helps you to absorb up essential information about the winemaking tradition. Visits frequently conclude with a sample of local wines.

Santorini is home to the Koutsogiannopoulos Wine Museum, where you may learn more about the wine culture and the wine-making process. Visiting it includes a one-of-a-kind wine-tasting experience. Make a reservation in advance!

CLASSICAL COOKING

Returning home with a few recipes to help you replicate the taste of your vacation is one of the finest ways to keep your memories alive!

Visitors can enjoy delicious Greek starters, savor locally produced wine, and participate in hands-on cooking courses to ensure that the finest keepsakes are the recipes they learn - this is why culinary excursions in Santorini are so popular!

Participants in the Cooking Class and Wine Tasting Tour gain new culinary expertise and methods, as well as a deeper understanding of viniculture through a visit to the volcanic vineyards. A professional chef will also assist you through the creation and execution of genuine Greek cuisine, the results of which you will be able to taste.

The Sunset Fishing Trip with Dinner and Drinks provides guests with a more realistic experience by allowing them to spend an evening on a traditional fishing boat.

Prepare to develop your fishing abilities and cook the day's catch on the balcony while admiring the crimson hues of the Aegean sunset!

We strongly advise reserving the culinary and wine trips prior to your arrival in Santorini, since they are quite popular.

SHOOTING PHOTOS

Santorini is a fantastic destination for amateur and professional photographers due to its postcard-like scenery, lovely villages, dreamy sunsets, and charming natural surroundings.

Many excursions in Santorini are centered on photography, allowing you to develop your pastime while visiting and discovering the island. During those tours, you will only see the most photogenic areas, both popular and hidden.

The Evening Photography Workshop is a photography program aimed for beginners where you can master the fundamentals of night photography. This course allows you to photograph the volcanic terrain at night and acquire some breathtaking images of the moonlit caldera.

The Photography Expedition is also available in the morning and afternoon. Whether you are a skilled photographer or not, you will be brought to several locations to improve your talents during this session.

JET SKI ADVENTURE

A jet ski adventure in Santorini ensures an out-of-the-ordinary experience, allowing you to combine your favorite watersport with an exploration of the volcanic coastline.

The Jet Ski Safari is an excellent choice for thrill enthusiasts. Participants can choose between a relaxed safari led tour and a jet ski rental. The second option gives you the freedom to explore the southern bays on your own.

There are more than five different jet ski safari expeditions to choose from. Consider combining them for a comprehensive sea exploration! It is best to book your jet ski safari in advance because they sell out rapidly.

SEA KAYAKING

Sea kayaking is a less risky but as enjoyable alternative to jet skiing. The Sea Kayaking and Snorkeling with Lunch tour provides a wonderful day in the sea away from the crowded lanes of the caldera settlements. Participants will have the opportunity to tour the southern portion of Santorini and its fascinating volcanic seashores. Swimming and snorkeling stops in the morning sun are provided. Lunch will be served at a traditional local tavern, where you will sample authentic Greek dishes.

On the shoreline, there are a plethora of extra activities. Scuba diving, parasailing, stand up paddling, and kitesurfing are just a few of the numerous possibilities available to watersports aficionados throughout their visit.

Visitors who are not interested in watersports may be interested in horseback riding, which provides unrivaled views of the caldera.

TOURS FROM OTHER NEXT-DOOR ISLANDS

Day trips to Santorini are offered from neighboring islands, allowing passengers to spend the entire day seeing the island's magnificent spots. The Tour from Paros and the Tour from Naxos, for example, are traveler favorites that include transportation to the greatest caldera settlements.

Chapter 16: Exploring the Enchanting Village of Oia

Every year, thousands of travelers are drawn to the timeless beauty of Santorini, Greece. As a result, it is no surprise that the island is one of the world's most popular tourist attractions. The island's untamed volcanic environment, rocky cliffs, wild nature, and magnificent beaches, along with its rich history and traditions, make it the jewel of Greece.

Santorini's distinctive half-moon shape was formed by a massive volcanic eruption around 1,650 BC. Its shape was circular in ancient times, and legend has it that the island miraculously emerged from the water. The powerful volcanic eruption, however, devastated almost half of the island, blanketed the Minoan colony of Akrotiri in ash, and generated waves so high that they reached the northern coastlines of Crete and demolished Minoan settlements, including the famous Knossos Palace.

Today, half of the caldera is submerged, making it the world's only sunken caldera. The volcano is still active, and several eruptions have occurred over the years. The most recent was in 1956, when little volcanic islets rose from the caldera's bottom. The islet of Nea Kameni appeared in one of these eruptions, close opposite the caldera communities. The volcano is a must-see in Santorini and may be reached by boat or jet ski tours.

Another enthralling sight in Santorini is the architecture of the settlements, which are situated close on the edge of the caldera. The sugar-cube cottages, paved streets, beautiful churches, and, most importantly, the spectacular view of the Aegean Sea define these lovely settlements. Indeed, the island's stunning architecture makes it an ideal venue for parkour, a new and remarkable sport. The most romantic sunset ever, with the orange sun dipping into the sea, can be seen from Oia. Because of its distinct environment, the island has become a favorite wedding and honeymoon destination.

The beauty of Santorini has inspired numerous writers and artists, as well as filmmakers, who frequently film on the island. Jules Verne visited the island on one of his voyages and discusses it in his novel Twenty Thousand Leagues Under the Sea. The island also inspired his novel The Mysterious Island, in which Captain Nemo and his crew saw a volcanic explosion. In the 1960s, Greek poet George Seferis penned a poem on Santorini, while globally renowned composer Yanni made a magnificent composition inspired by the island.

Many people associate Santorini with the mythological Atlantis, yet this theory is now considered to be a myth. Apart from trekking around the caldera towns, the beautiful beaches on the island's southern side, including as Red Beach, Kamari, and Perissa, which have developed into huge beach resorts, are well worth a visit.

What should I know before going?
- The caldera villages of Imerovigli and Oia provide the most spectacular views.
- Make time to explore the volcano and wineries.
- Take in Santorini's sunrise and sunset.
- The eastern and southern parts of Santorini have the best bays.
- Rent a car for convenient transportation.
- Santorini fills up quickly during the summer, so plan ahead of time.
- Island hopping is ideal if you have more than three days off.

What size is the island?
Santorini is a small island in terms of land area, with only roughly 76 square kilometers. Thirasia island and the other nearby islets are part of the Municipality of Thira (not to be confused with Fira, Santorini's capital).

How many people do you think dwell there?
Santorini has a permanent population of about 15,500 people, while the island receives approximately 2 million visitors each year.

During the tourist season, many seasonal workers stay in Santorini and work in the tourism and hospitality industries.

Except for Thirasia, the smaller islets near Santorini's crescent-shaped caldera that are also part of the volcanic complex are all uninhabited.

Is it possible to visit in one or two days?

One day in Santorini is insufficient, especially if you come by ferry after a lengthy travel. It is strongly advised to spend at least three full days visiting the main sights and attractions. Determine the number of days required for your visit.

How long should I stay on vacation?

The best time to visit Santorini is between three and five days. You can tour the main sights in three days if you stick to a rigid timetable. The availability of five days ensures comfort and a lighter schedule.

How much money do I require?

During the high season, Santorini is fairly pricy. If you intend to eat and drink out, a daily budget of €150 per person should be considered. To keep costs down, you might incorporate some free and low-cost activities into your program.

Why is the island so pricey?

Santorini is relatively pricey because it has been a tourist destination for decades due to its buried Caldera, Volcano, and breathtaking sunsets. More than 1.5 million visitors visit it each year, and the caldera establishments have grown dramatically. The island has acquired a lavish appearance and is promoted internationally as a must-see Greek island.

When is island hopping the best option?

When you have more than four days of vacation, island hopping from Santorini is a terrific addition to your itinerary. It is not suggested for less days, however, because you will have to rush through it and hence will not be able to appreciate it fully.

Is the island safe to visit?

Santorini, like the other Cycladic islands, is extremely safe. Petty crime is uncommon and mostly committed by other visitors, so simply having your bag and personal stuff on you is sufficient. If you leave your wallet or pocketbook in a business, the personnel will hold it until you return.

What is the meaning of the name Santorini?

Surprisingly, the contemporary name "Santorini" was founded by the Crusaders in the 13th century. The island is named after a modest church dedicated to Saint Irene in Perissa. The name is derived from the combination of 'Santa Irini'.

Is Santorini suitable for couples?

Because of the spectacular and romantic sunset vistas of the Caldera towns, Santorini is ideal for couples, honeymooners, vow renewal, and proposing to your significant other. In fact, most hotels provide honeymoon suites and special arrangements for couples.

Is it windy in Santorini?

During July and August, Santorini is influenced by the seasonal Meltemi wind. Meltemi is a strong northern wind that can be very advantageous for windsurfing and kitesurfing but should be avoided for lengthy boat rides in medium or small vessels due to the risk of seasickness. When it's windy, a light jacket and a hairband are all you need.

What is it like to visit Santorini?

Santorini is a beautiful Cycladic island in the southern Aegean Sea with breathtaking volcanic landscapes and world-renowned sunset views. It is a luxury-oriented location ideal for couples, with a rich viticulture and history to explore.

Is it possible to travel directly to Santorini?

Many European countries, including France, Germany, Spain, and the United Kingdom, offer direct flights to Santorini's international airport. However, there are no direct flights from North America to Santorini. Find out more about the flights.

What is the best way to get from Athens to Santorini?

Domestic flights from Eleftherios Venizelos International Airport connect Athens to Santorini, as do daily ferry routes from the ports of Piraeus and Rafina. During the tourist season, ferry routes become more frequent. Find out more about how to get there.

How can I travel on a budget?

- Avoid visiting during peak season because every facility is pricey.
- Reserve a lodging far from the Caldera communities.
- Hike alone from Oia to Fira.
- Take public transit.
- For a few days, rent a bike instead of a car.
- Swim in unorganized bays and avoid booking a sunbed.
- Instead of eating out, buy groceries and prepare your own lunch.
- Instead of scheduling a guided wine and walking tour, go on your own.

Chapter 17: Exploring Santorini's Charming Villages

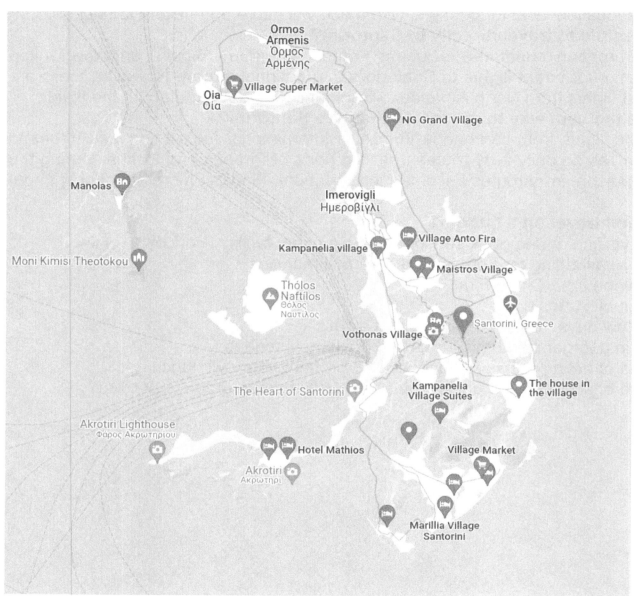

Santorini is home to a number of lovely villages, each with its own distinct history, architecture, and attractions. Oia, famed for its spectacular sea views and beautiful sunsets; Fira, the island's capital and a famous tourist destination for its active nightlife, shopping, and restaurants; and Pyrgos, a lovely village with panoramic views and old buildings, are among the most popular communities.

Other notable villages include Imerovigli, which is known for its panoramic views of the caldera; Akrotiri, which is home to an important archaeological site; Megalochori, a traditional village with beautiful old houses; and Perissa and Kamari, which are known for their stunning black sand beaches and a fishing port with a white sandy beach, respectively. From beaches and magnificent vistas to gastronomy and local culture, each community has something special to offer visitors.

Santorini is a popular tourist destination and a perfect site to discover and experience Greece's natural beauty, rich history, and culture.

Fira, Santorini

Fira is the island's gorgeous capital as well as its largest and most cosmopolitan settlement. It is located on the western edge of the island, opposite the volcano and the two volcanic islands in the sea, Palaia Kammeni and Nea Kammeni.

For those preferring a more traditional experience, access to Fira is also possible via cable car or a donkey trail from the port, in addition to road routes from the port and airport.

Fira is a mix of natural beauty, social life, nightlife, and shopping, where you can experience the island's vibrancy and where all the action happens. The Caldera vista, which leaves visitors awestruck at any time of day, is what makes it so appealing. A stroll through the gorgeous lanes during the day will fill you with peace, while at night you may find yourself in the midst of a large party. There are numerous restaurants, cafes, bars, and clubs where you may relax and enjoy the spectacular view or dance and have a good time. It actually possesses the island's best dining and entertainment options, as well as the largest shopping area. Furthermore, there are numerous clothing stores, gift shops, tourist shops, supermarkets, and other conveniences.

Among the magnificent monuments are the Megaro Gyzi Cultural Center, which houses a range of collections and hosts a variety of cultural events such as concerts and theatrical plays, as well as Fira's two cathedrals. The Archaeological Museum of Thera and the Museum of Prehistoric Thera, both of which provide a wealth of antiquities and historic things from the entire island, are also located in Fira. In addition, in Kontochori village, close to Fira, there is the Folklore Museum of Emmanuel A. Lignos, which houses six rooms-exhibitions depicting life in the twentieth century.

The city of Santorini has a plethora of lodging alternatives, ranging from fancy hotels with spectacular caldera views to a camping area for an alternative stay that will satisfy nature enthusiasts.

Oia - Santorini

Oia, also known as Pano Meria, is regarded Santorini's most attractive hamlet and the most popular destination for sunset viewing, as it offers a fantastic view of the well-known sunset, possibly the most renowned sunset in the world. It is located on the caldera slope on Santorini's northwest coast.

It's no surprise that a few movies have been shot in Oia, given its breathtaking beauty. It is a fusion of white-blue buildings and churches with pink and ocher decorations "hanging" from the caldera, creating a beautiful painting that is impossible to describe. It is a pretty tranquil and idyllic community that comes alive around sunset.

The sunset in Oia has a completely different meaning. It is the time of day when you can discover something new. Visitors and residents alike congregate in the streets, stairwells, and roofs to enjoy the sunset. It's like a giant party that happens every evening and concludes when everyone in the room claps their hands together as the sun sets in the sea. The sunset colors complement Oia's amazing beauty and provide a spectacular spectacle.

In Oia, you may walk through the picturesque little streets, explore stores and galleries, and dine in the atmospheric cafes, pubs, and restaurants. Ammoudi Bay, at the bottom of the hamlet, has a row of traditional pubs by the shore serving local cuisine. If you walk the small trail that leads to a unique diving location, you can swim in magnificent crystal waters with a breathtaking caldera view above you.

In terms of attractions, Oia is home to one of Santorini's top museums. The Naval Maritime Museum features one of the most extensive collections in Greece, depicting the island's naval history. Aside from its history, the ruins of Agios Nikolaos Castle are a popular location for sunset gazing. In Oia, you can visit one of the island's wineries and sample the delicious local wine. Finally, your gaze would be drawn to the distinctive windmill that ornaments the village.

Oia is easily accessible by vehicle or bus from Fira, and the drive provides a spectacular view. In Oia, there are numerous hotels, villas, mansions, and flats to suit every taste.

Imerovigli - Santorini

Imerovigli, commonly known as "The Aegean's Balcony," is located on the highest point of the caldera cliffs, roughly 300 meters above sea level. It is located in the north of the island, 3 kilometers from Fira, the capital. Its location affords a spectacular view of the renowned volcano, the beautiful Aegean Sea, and an out-of-this-world sunset.

The village's most remarkable feature is the iconic, massive rock known as Skaros, which located on the seaward side. It is extremely important because it was the most important of Santorini's five strongholds. It was previously an observation point that provided security against pirates. Today, visitors may see the ruins of the 1817 earthquake as well as the breathtaking panorama from the top. Hiking is also available at Skaros, the symbol of Santorini.

In Imerovigli, there are various churches and chapels, including the prominent church of Panagia Malteza and the chapel of Panagia Theoskepasti, which is built on the cliff edge in front of Skaros and offers a unique panoramic view of the caldera. In addition, the female monastery of Agios Nikolaos, located between the villages of Imerovigli and Firostefani, houses a folklore museum as well as an ecclesiastical museum with rare Byzantine icons.

Imerovigli is an excellent alternative for a secluded, romantic getaway filled with peace and quiet. It creates a stunning panorama of whitewashed homes, flowers, and cobblestone alleys. You may escape the noise and bustle by strolling around the tranquil, concrete trails. It promises precious, calm moments as well as an unbeatable view. Relax at the classic taverns, restaurants, and cafes with beautiful terraces.

In Imerovigli, you may stay in five-star hotels, villas, premium resorts with swimming pools perched on the cliff edge, as well as tiny family-run hotels, studios, apartments, and rooms to let.

Imerovigli is easily accessible from Fira by vehicle, taxi, bus, or on foot if you prefer to stroll.

Firostefani - Santorini

Firostefani village is considered a separate settlement, however it is essentially an extension of Fira, Santorini's city. The name "Firostefani" (Fira + Stefani, meaning "crown" in Greek) comes from its location on Fira's highest point. Its spectacular setting on the caldera in the northwestern section of the island makes it a must-see.

The view from Fira's crown is pretty stunning, providing visitors with a distinct viewpoint of the volcano. The natural beauty of the caldera, combined with the perspective of the volcano, creates a breathtaking spectacle. A stroll through the tiny, picturesque lanes will undoubtedly bring you joy. You may spend many beautiful hours admiring the scenery, especially when the sun sets. Of course, the view of the village might awe you again at night, when the lights make it look like a masterpiece.

There are numerous white-blue churches scattered among the gorgeous, traditional residences that will catch your eye. There are a few modest restaurants and cafes placed on beautiful sites in this medieval village that will make you feel welcome. Some shops and mini markets are also available to supply you with the necessities, with the majority of them centered on the main shopping street. Firostefani's main advantage is its proximity to Santorini's city; it is only a short distance from the packed and boisterous Fira. As a result, it creates the ideal equation. Serenity and tranquility may coexist with a vibrant nightlife.

Close by, between Firostefani and Imerovigli, is the Agios Nikolaos female monastery, which houses a folklore museum and an ecclesiastical museum with rare Byzantine icons and a unique icon of the Saint Nicholas.

Firostefani offers numerous residential alternatives. Luxurious hotels, suites, villas, apartments, and rooms with breathtaking views to meet every requirement. The calming environment that pervades every aspect of the village makes it an appealing option.

Pyrgos - Santorini

Pyrgos is unique in that it is the tallest village on the island, affording spectacular views of both sides of the island. It is located on the west shore, approximately 8 kilometers southeast of Fira, Santorini's city.

Because of its fortunate location, it shines out from afar, and the view from up there offers a unique perspective that you can only see from Pyrgos. You can see green slopes, the big sea, and the entire island unroll beneath your feet. Pyrgos maintains its traditional Cycladic architecture. It's adorable since it's partly undeveloped, with small, twisting alleys and stone buildings.

Pyrgos is surrounded by vineyards and blue-domed churches. As you wind your way through the different uphill and downhill alleys, you'll come across modest galleries and businesses tucked into hidden corners. At the bottom of the town, there are some tourist shops, mini markets, welcome restaurants and taverns serving great food, and coffee shops, the majority of which are centered on the main, round square.

As you ascend this hillside settlement, you will come across the Venetian Kasteli, one of Santorini's five castles, with an unrivaled outlook. It's built amphitheatrically, with three churches within and outside. On the west side is the church Theotoki or Koimisis of Theotokou, which is thought to be one of the island's oldest. The

Eisodion of Theotokou church is located on Kasteli's highest level, and the church of Agia Theodosia is extremely close to its entrance.

Many additional churches and chapels may be found in Pyrgos, but the monastery of Profitis Ilias, located close the hamlet, is noteworthy. The museum of "The icons and relics Collection" of Pyrgos is held inside the chapel of Agia Triada (of Profitis Ilias) and includes an important collection of ecclesiastical goods, literature, and other art works.

Furthermore, at Pyrgos, you may tour vineyards, learn about the history and production of the famous Santorini wine, and, most importantly, taste the surprisingly tasty wine.

In Pyrgos, you may stay in welcoming residences, friendly hotels, villas, and suites that will amaze you with their breathtaking views.

Kamari - Santorini

Kamari is a beach village on Santorini's southeastern shore, near the north foot of Mesa Vouno mountain, a few kilometers from the city. It is easily accessible by bus, taxi, or rental car. It gets its name from a tiny arch on the south end of the beach that was part of an ancient Poseidon shrine.

The community features contemporary infrastructure and a plethora of services, as well as Santorini's airport. There is a lengthy promenade with stores, restaurants, taverns, and cafe-bars where you can relax and enjoy the sea wind. You will also get the opportunity to listen to live traditional Greek music. Furthermore, Kamari is home to the island's sole cinemas, one of which is a stunning open-air cinema surrounded by woods.

The primary draw is the Kamari beach, the most popular on the island and the only one to have been given the Blue Flag. It is spotless and well-kept, with deck chairs, umbrellas, and lifeguards. It stretches for miles beneath the intriguing mountain, boasting crystal clear waters and unusual black sand and pebbles. Without a question, it makes for a spectacular sight. There is a scuba diving school for courses and snorkeling, and you can also try out other water activities.

An important element of history can be found on the top of Mesa Vouno. The archaeological site of Ancient Thera is a significant feature of Santorini, with temples, ancient graves, buildings, and the theater awe you, as will the breathtaking vista.

The Wine Museum in Vothonas hamlet, on the route to Kamari, showcases wine machines and instruments and explains the history and method of wine manufacturing. In addition, you can pay a visit to one of the best wineries, which provides tours of the facilities and, most importantly, a pleasurable experience.

In terms of lodging, there are numerous five-star hotels as well as less priced flats and rooms to rent to suit every taste and budget.

Akrotiri - Santorini

Akrotiri is a quiet village, not as popular or developed as other villages, but of considerable interest and significance. It is located on the south-western coast of Santorini, about 15 kilometers from Fira, and offers breathtaking views of the island. Because of its geographical location, Akrotiri is a genuine promontory. It is famed for its lighthouse, which is one of the best in Greece and from which you can enjoy magnificent sunsets.

In Akrotiri, you can discover two wonderful beaches that are unlike any other and form an impressive landscape. The view in Red Beach will leave you speechless. It is encircled by reddish, steep rocks that create a stunning contrast with the dark blue sea. A wild scene with large red boulders in the water and red stones all over the beach. The second is White Beach, a small, lovely beach surrounded by towering, white rocks and covered in white pebbles. They aren't easily accessible, yet that only adds to their charm.

Akrotiri village is home to two historical gems that are the village's principal attractions. One of these is the archaeological site of Akrotiri, a significant prehistoric Aegean town that is well worth a visit. It is possible to stroll inside it and see frescoes, relics, objects, furniture, advanced drainage systems, and even multi-story Bronze Age buildings.

The other is the Castle of Akrotiri, also known as La Ponta, which was one of Santorini's five fortified villages. A 13th century tower (Goulas) in the heart of the Venetian fortress offers a beautiful outlook. Today, the ruins can be admired, as well as the display and workshop of traditional musical instruments. Some evenings, music events are also scheduled, which is a terrific way to spend your time in Akrotiri.

Akrotiri has a few residential alternatives with spectacular views of the caldera and volcano. There are hotels, villas, and suites with beautiful swimming pools as well as more basic rooms, so there is something for everyone. Akrotiri may be reached by vehicle or by bus from Fira.

Perissa - Santorini

Perissa is a beach community on the island's southeastern tip, 13 kilometers from the capital. It is located at the southern base of Mesa Vouno mountain and is thought to be the site of the ancient city of Elefsina.

Most visitors come to Perissa to enjoy the magnificent beach, which is distinguished by deep, dark blue waves and black lava sand. It has been awarded the Blue Flag for its excellent organization, which includes sunbeds, umbrellas, beach bars, lifeguards, and a playground. There are also water sports facilities, diving centers, a water park, and a beach volley area to enhance your experience. Perissa beach connects to Perivolos, and there are numerous nightclubs, restaurants, taverns, and cafes to pick from for fun day and night. There are little markets and other shops throughout the village that sell clothing, souvenirs, and other necessities.

The remains of Ancient Thera town, a renowned archeological site with numerous eminent structures, are located on the summit of the mountain Mesa Vouno. Apart from its historical significance, it is worth visiting for the spectacular views of Perissa and Kamari villages.

The Museum of Thera's Minerals and Fossils, which opened in 2006 in Perissa, is a must-see. Inside, you may see fascinating minerals and fossils from not only Thera, but also the rest of Greece and other nations. The museum contains exhibits that can transport you 1,5 billion years back in time and deepen your understanding of the evolution of man and all forms of life.

You can visit various prominent churches and chapels in Perissa village, which are comparable to the beauty of the island. The church of Holy Cross, one of Santorini's largest churches, is located in Perissa's center plaza. The modest, white washed chapel of Panagia Katefiani, erected on the slopes of Mesa Vouno mountain and built on an immense rock, offers a spectacular view. Finally, at the foot of the mountain, you may examine the ruins of the Basilica of Agia Irini, which is apparently where the island got its name.

It is easily accessible by car or bus and boasts numerous magnificent hotels and villas, comfortable flats, studios, and even a campsite for a pleasant stay.

Chapter 18: Exploring Museums in Santorini

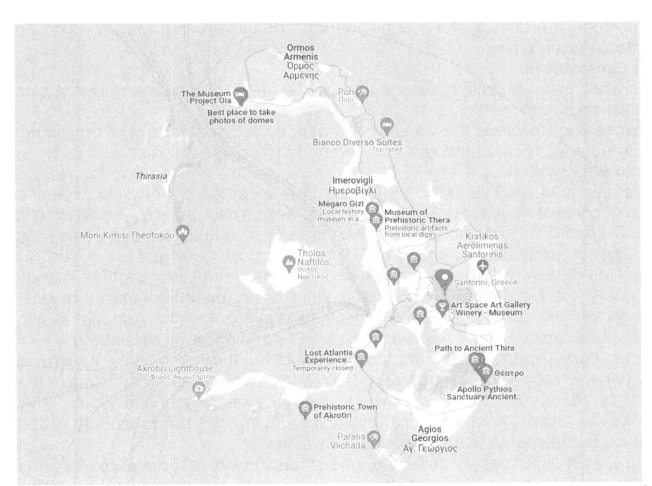

The island of Santorini has an archeological treasure that tourists, particularly those interested in history and culture, can appreciate and learn about in the many excellent museums. Santorini has numerous museums distributed among its picturesque villages. They display noteworthy discoveries that demonstrate the island's lengthy history and prominent presence. Santorini's rich tradition is portrayed in priceless collections that include rare and important exhibits.

The Archaeological Museum and the Museum of Prehistoric Thera are two important museums that house extraordinary artifacts and treasures from the island's excavations. The Argyros Mansion, a prominent neoclassical mansion, has been renovated into a museum transporting tourists to the nineteenth century. The Folklore Museum is another gem, with an antique vineyard, a library, an art gallery, and a magnificent church. The Naval Maritime Museum depicts Santorini's naval history through literature, records, and nautical equipment. The Icons and Relics Collection features rare ecclesiastical treasures from the 16th, 17th, and 18th centuries. A distinct museum is the Minerals and Fossils Museum, which houses priceless specimens from Greece and around the world. The Wine Museum offers amazing multi-purpose excursions where guests may taste and learn more about the renowned Santorini product.

These and other gems on the island are unquestionably worth a visit as they reveal Santorini's historic history, enriching your understanding and providing an unforgettable experience.

Akrotiri Excavations

The excavations in Akrotiri revealed one of the Aegean's most important and spectacular prehistoric settlements.

A vast archeological site in the village of Akrotiri, on the south coast of the island, is considered a significant geological discovery. Let's go into its past!

Historical information

The excavations at Akrotiri, which began in 1967 under the supervision of famed Greek archeologist Spyridon Marinatos and were resumed by archaeologist Christos Doumas in 1974, made the prehistoric site of Akrotiri famous across the world. However, excavations began in 1870 by the French geologist F. Fouque.

Archeologists discovered traces of human settlement at the historic site of Akrotiri dating back to the Neolithic Age (4500 BC), when the hamlet grew from a modest fishing and farming community to become very significant in the Aegean trading business. the strategic location between Cyprus and Minoan Crete made it a vital stop in the copper trade, which aided in the development of the society. According to the pottery recovered, Akrotiri people had trade links with Crete, the Dodecanese, Greece's mainland, Cyprus, and maybe Egypt and Syria. This trading activity aided the civilization's expansion, increased the prosperity of the city, and led the residents to a prosperous way of life.

Agriculture, animal husbandry, fisheries, and shipping were all important elements in this growth. The digs also reveal the occupants' jobs as engineers, architects, town planners, builders, and even artists. Wheat, barley, legumes, olives, and vineyards were among their crops, and they exported wine, metals, and volcanic rocks. Residents were also involved in beekeeping and, in particular, weaving and saffron harvesting.

The residents' high standard of life enabled them to display their artistic abilities and talents. Archaeologists discovered a wide range of vessels manufactured by locals, in a variety of sizes, forms, and colors, for both domestic and aesthetic purposes.

Large murals were also discovered, demonstrating the Minoans' impact and serving as a vital source of knowledge about their way of life at the time. They were discovered in large and tiny walls, doors, and windows, and reflect nature, religion, and daily life.

Akrotiri's prosperous culture met an untimely end around 1613 BC, when one of the most violent volcanic eruptions and a huge earthquake occurred, burying the town under volcanic ash. This aided in the preservation of the settlement's ruins. The eruption was so powerful that it altered the morphology of Santorini and linked it to the story of Lost Atlantis, however this has yet to be proven scientifically. Fortunately, no human remains have been discovered, as the inhabitants were forced to flee following a series of powerful earthquakes.

How does one go to the Akrotiri archaeological site?

Visitors can now wander around the city's ruins, admiring the narrow stone-paved streets and the ruins of the large squares, mud and stone houses, and basements used as storage and workshops, while some of the significant objects discovered are on display at the Museum of Prehistoric Thera in Fira. Some notable wall murals can also be seen in Athens' National Archaeological Museum.

Akrotiri's prehistoric site is a 20-minute drive from Fira and is easily accessible by vehicle or public transportation. If you choose to visit the location by automobile, there is a parking lot nearby, as well as the famed Red Beach, which is well worth a visit. Public transit from Fira is fairly frequent, and an updated bus timetable is available at the Fira main bus station.

Another option for visiting this beautiful settlement is to take one of the many bus tours offered on the island. You can select between guided tours and tours that involve visiting all of Santorini's most gorgeous and well-known locations while moving about in the convenience of having everything prepared for you.

Ancient Thera

Ancient Thera, which represents a vast ancient civilization, is associated with the second most important historic period in Santorini's history. Mesa Vouno Mountain, which sits east of Prophet Elias Mountain and divides the seaside communities of Perissa and Kamari, is home to Ancient Thera. It is approximately 365 meters high, making it a great observation point on the southern Aegean Sea, and its steep slopes provide natural defense. This advantageous location was excellent for the Lacedaemonian colonists to establish their town. They arrived in the eighth century BC, accompanied by their king Theras, and called the island Thera after him. There were also many building materials and the island's only natural springs at this location. This fortified location was later appreciated by the Ptolemaic dynasty, and it became Egypt's naval and military base in the 4th century BC.

The excavations at Mesa Vouno Mountain, which began in 1896 by a German baron and were completed in 1961 by Greek archaeologists, discovered a Hellenistic Period village. A large paved road, numerous smaller walkways, and a drainage system were all there. The public structures were made of limestone, whereas the private structures were made of small, asymmetrical stones. Two graves, a theater, markets, pagan temples, Christian churches, baths, and other public buildings have also been uncovered, indicating a sophisticated civilization in which religion was significant. Thera was the island's ecclesiastical and commercial center.

Because the Spartans were a conservative people who did not support the development of arts and education, art was not widely cultivated. However, archaeological digs have uncovered outstanding ceramics and plastic arts items. Despite its abstinence and conservatism, it was influenced by cultural advancements and maintained trading relations with the rest of the Cycladic islands, northern Aegean islands, Crete, Cyprus, mainland Greece, Corinth, and even North Africa. Furthermore, Thera was among the first to use the Phoenician alphabet as the basis for Greek writing. A lengthy period of drought prompted the people of Thera to establish their unique colony in Africa, the Ancient City of Cyrene, in 630 BC, which was a magnificent society that excelled in arts and education.

The ancient city of Thera saw both brilliant and terrible moments over the years, as it was occupied and conquered by many civilizations. Its collapse began at the end of the third century AD, when citizens began to migrate to the island's coastlines, which provided a more comfortable way of life.

Visitors can experience this bygone magnificence today by exploring a substantial portion of Ancient Thera that has been unearthed. A visit to the archeological site on Mesa Vouno Mountain also affords breathtaking views of the beautiful Aegean Sea. In addition, the Archaeological Museum of Fira houses a large collection of statues, clay figurines, pots, vases, and other objects and artifacts that are well worth seeing for their unusual finds. Finally, the National Archaeological Museum in Athens houses the Apollo of Thera kouros (ancient Greek statue of a young man) from the 6th century BC. Two more, dating from the 7th century BC, can be found in Fira's Archaeological Museum.

Wine Museum Koutsogiannopoulos

In Vothonas village, there is a very unusual underground museum dedicated to the history of wine in Santorini!

The Wine Museum is built in a natural cave eight meters below ground and spans a 300-meter-long labyrinth.

The museum took 21 years to complete and was entirely funded by the Koutsoyannopoulos family, members of which used to be vine-growers. The museum is now administered by the fourth-generation owners and winemakers, whose enthusiasm for wine is unwavering.

The significance of its existence stems from the fact that the rich volcanic soil of Santorini is intertwined with its superb wine types. That is also why Santorini has a lengthy winemaking legacy, with its wines earning global acclaim for their excellent flavors, making them the most famous local product! The Koutsoyannopoulos family wants to carry on the tradition, preserve the history, and share their passion for winemaking.

Through engaging exhibitions, the Wine Museum provides an insight into the history of wine and the lives of vintners in Santorini from 1660 to 1970. It includes intriguing aspects such as sound effects, still-life arrangements, and partially mobile figures that eloquently depict the history and process of winemaking. Furthermore, real machinery, tools, and containers, including some rare pieces, are grouped and shown in historical order. Similarly, the many phases of winemaking are displayed in a way that allows guests to actively engage with them during the tour, from trimming and plowing to harvesting, stomping, and grape weighing.

Throughout the year, the museum provides a self-guided tour to the general public, which includes an automated audio guide in 14 languages and a booklet. The tour concludes at the office of Grigorios Koutsoyannopoulos, the family winery's founder, where guests may explore his personal items dating back to 1870. Following the walk, the event moves to a wine-tasting room. Visitors can enjoy a wine-tasting adventure by experiencing four of the family winery's top wines! Finally, guests can watch a movie about Santorini's extensive history, way of life, and the evolution of wine production on the island.

Aside from the Wine Museum, which provides the most accurate picture of traditional Greek winemaking, the family still controls the winery, which was founded in 1870, that produces the legendary Volcan Wines and is a leading producer in Santorini. The winery's indoor and outdoor areas are also accessible for organizing various events, including weddings. Furthermore, unique events with live music or a DJ (traditional Greek music is suggested), wonderful cuisine, and, of course, the finest variety of Volcan Wines can be organized.

The Wine Museum, which is unique in Greece and one of the best in the world, provides an unforgettable experience because it is so much more than a museum!

Thera Prehistoric Museum

The stunning Museum of Prehistoric Thera, located in Fira, the city of Santorini, is one of Greece's most prominent museums. It is housed in a cutting-edge, two-story structure, the construction of which began in the early 1970s and was completed in 2000. Professor Spyridon Marinatos, a prominent Greek archeologist who led excavations at the archaeological site of Akrotiri and prompted the establishment of a museum to house the valuable finds from this major urban center that came to light, where a prominent regional civilization of the prehistoric world used to thrive during the Minoan Bronze Age, was the museum's proponent.

The finds on display at the Prehistoric Museum of Thera come from various excavations on the island, such as at the settlements of Akrotiri and Potamos, rescue excavations at various sites on the island, and some objects discovered by chance or handed over. The exhibits, which span from the Late Neolithic Era to the Cycladic Periods, are in great shape. Visitors can see the growth of Thera in the Prehistoric Times unfold before their eyes in the displays, which bear witness to a magnificent course that made Thera one of the most important islands in the Aegean during the 18th and 17th centuries BC.

The museum is open daily (except Tuesdays in winter) and features temporary exhibitions on the ground floor as well as four permanent displays on the first floor. The first pertains to Thera's research history, the second to the island's geology, the third to the island's history from the Late Neolithic to the Late Cycladic I Period, and the final to the heyday of Akrotiri (mature Late Cycladic I Period, 17th century BC).

The Prehistoric Thera Museum can be thought of as an extension of the archaeological site of Akrotiri, where tourists can walk through the incredible, well-preserved prehistoric city, because it houses numerous artifacts from there, most notably the frescoes, the stunning mural paintings. These were discovered in both public and private structures in Akrotiri and form one of the museum's most spectacular exhibitions. They are colorful depictions of nature and everyday life that provide important insight into the manner of life and the surroundings at the time. There are also tools, utensils, marble figures, pottery, and some jewelry among the goods, indicating that the residents may have taken their valuables with them as they fled the island owing to the impending volcanic eruption.

The remaining collections, which are organized chronologically, include Neolithic, Early and Middle Cycladic pottery, Early Cycladic metal artifacts, and marble figures, which are among the museum's earliest pieces, as well as ancient items such as vases, ritual objects, and bird jugs. Finally, the museum has fossils of critters and plants that flourished before humans arrived on Thera, such as palm trees, olive leaves, and schinus.

Thera Archaeological Museum

An outstanding and highly interesting museum is located beside the cable car in Fira, the city of Santorini. The Archaeological Museum of Thera is a modest educational jewel that provides insight into the island's past and demonstrates how clever the civilizations that came before us were. The Ministry of Public Works built it in 1960 after the former one, completed in 1902, fell following the devastating earthquake of 1956.

The Archaeological Museum is open to the public daily from 8:00-15:00, except on Mondays, and is a fantastic destination for those who are interested in foreign cultures and want to learn about Santorini's history. Sculpture from the Archaic to the Roman Period, inscriptions from the Archaic to the Roman Period, and vases and clay figurines from the Geometric to the Hellenistic Periods are on show.

A substantial portion of the exhibits come from excavations on Mesa Vouno Mountain, where a Hellenistic Period village was unearthed. The majority of them were discovered in the antique Thera cemetery and include ceramic artifacts, jars, amphorae, and antique statues like as the emblematic nude male statue known as kouros. The rest of the discoveries can be seen at Athens' National Archaeological Museum. It is advised that visitors visit both the Ancient Thera archeological site and the archeological Museum to obtain a better understanding of the island's history and evolution.

Some of the most important artifacts on display are a Theran amphora with geometric decoration discovered in the archaic cemetery of Ancient Thera in the early 7th century BC, a volcanic boulder weighing 480 kg with an inscription about the athlete Eumastas who managed to lift it with his bare hands, and, finally, a krater with Attic black figures discovered in the second half of the 6th century BC. There are also some Byzantine works of art and an excellent collection of 5th century BC geometric ceramics. There have even been prehistoric findings from Akrotiri and Chistiana islet.

The spectacular exhibits and unique treasures of the Archaeological Museum of Thera will captivate all visitors as they travel back in time and witness the island's history unfold before their eyes. A visit here will also show the actual character of Santorini, as well as the fact that it is a varied island with many hidden treasures and a rich cultural past.

Folklore Museum of Emmanuel A. Lignos

The Santorini Folklore Museum is located in Kontochori village, near to the island's capital, Fira. Emmanuel A. Lignos, a lawyer, journalist, and editor of the monthly newspaper "Theraic News," founded it in 1974. The museum is housed in a traditional Santorini cave home, which was built in 1861, according to an inscription on the canava wall. The house's rooms, which survived the 1956 earthquake, were refurbished in 1973 and equipped with antique furniture, utensils, and antiques. In 1993, an addition to the original structure was erected to house an art gallery and various studios, as well as a chapel dedicated to the Saints Constantine and Helen in remembrance of the founder's uncle.

The layout of each chamber depicts the typical cave home of Santorini and illustrates life at the turn of the twentieth century. The house has a hall, two bedrooms, a dining room, a kitchen, and a cellar for food storage, as well as the distinctive arches and windows. There are barrels, antique utensils, equipment, treading vats, and a wine press where the famous Santorini wine was created in the typical domestic winery erected in a cavern. Visitors will find housewares, trinkets, pictures, and traditional costumes in each room. A phonograph and a pair of handcrafted wedding crowns stick out among the numerous household belongings. Furthermore, the museum has a collection of historical archives that include folders containing articles on Santorini, rare images of the island dating back to 1895, old and new rare books about Santorini, lithographs, maps, and important manuscripts.

A beautiful courtyard and a garden with trees and flowers surround the home, where the charming church dedicated to Saints Constantine and Helen was built. It has a belfry and a celebrations chamber, and it highlights local religious traditions. Guests can examine an exhibition of sketches, oil paintings, watercolors, and other works inspired by Santorini at the Museum Gallery, a wing erected later to the main home. Finally, the Folklore Museum contains many traditional workshops for carpenters, barrel makers, shoemakers, and tinsmiths.

A visit to the museum is a trip back in time that provides important insight into the culture and traditions of the island of Santorini. The museum, which is one of Greece's most prominent Folklore Museums, is the result of Emmanuel A. Lignos' efforts and urge to promote and raise awareness of Santorini's cultural legacy. It is open to the public from 10:00-16:00 Monday through Friday.

Maritime Museum

The excellent Naval Maritime Museum, located in the lovely village of Oia, provides insight into local and Greek naval history in general. The museum was founded in 1956 by Captain Antonis Dakoronias and has been housed in a beautiful captain home donated by Dina Manolessou-Birbili since 1990. It is a two-story mansion that has been repaired and converted into the current museum. Oia owns many captain residences, which are remnants of the village's prior prosperous heyday.

The Oia Museum, which is available to the public daily except Tuesdays, is a "window" into a time when Santorini was a thriving island thanks to shipping and played an important role in Greece's nautical history as an integral part of her great navy. It gives excellent information about the intriguing growth of Greek shipping as well as aspects of life in the Cyclades through its exhibits, which have been collected since 1951.

Santorini's considerable contribution to the Greek Navy was significant for the island's economic prosperity, which was dependent on its merchant fleet. The island's nautical commerce peaked in the late nineteenth and early twentieth centuries. Santorini owned many vessels with considerable tonnage that traveled from Alexandria to Russia, crossing the Eastern Mediterranean and exporting Santorini's renowned wine and pumice stones from its volcanic terrain. The captains returned with a variety of things, including grain, cherry tomatoes, china, cotton, textiles, timber, and furniture, but they also obtained valuable knowledge, experiences, and fortune.

Visitors to the museum's ground floor can view nautical equipment and tools, as well as a brief description of their usage, such as compasses, maps, sextants, portholes, hanging hurricane lamps, log meters, propellers, anchors, pulleys, deadeyes, and more. A manual driller and a large foot driven lathe in great shape are among the most impressive items on show. Visitors will also be impressed by the library, which houses rare books and documents, delivery dockets, logbooks, and nautical maps.

On the first floor, there are old and new ship models, mariners' chests, uniforms, pictures of local captains, and unusual figureheads. Finally, the Naval Maritime Museum's excellent collection includes a wide range of impressive aquarelles showcasing historic sailing vessels as well as rare images of families, personnel, and vessels that bring to life an era when Santorini was a bustling island.

The Argyros Mansion

This estate provides great insight into Greek culture and customs while gently resurrecting a period of affluence that played an important role in Santorini's history!

The village of Messaria, where the mansion is located, used to have a significant position among the island's settlements as a prominent winemaking center and an affluent community with scores of magnificent manor houses. It now has an aristocratic air about it, but just a few homes remain to remind one of its previous magnificence. Only the Argyros Mansion is open to the public.

The home was erected in 1888 by local craftsmen for the wealthy landowner and wine merchant George Argyros. It was a magnificent neoclassical home with outstanding architecture and elegance. However, following the devastating earthquake of 1956, the building sustained damage and a portion of it fell. As a result, it was abandoned for the next 35 years, until the Greek Ministry of Culture pronounced it a masterpiece and a notable example of architecture in 1985. Its refurbishment began in 1987 and was finished in 1994 with outstanding results. It was also named a Greek cultural heritage site by the Europa Nostra Award in 1997.

Manolis Argyros, the current owner and fourth generation of the family, opened the doors of the mansion, which now serves as a museum, to the public. The museum, located on the first floor of the mansion, allows visitors to appreciate the beauty of Santorini in the nineteenth century, feel the ambiance of a renowned bygone era, and learn about undiscovered elements of life on the island. Guests can tour the mansion's rooms and observe noteworthy hand-made furniture from around the world, everyday items, and exquisite nuances in the décor, such as admirable paintings. The beautiful oak floors, bright hues, and ceiling paintings of extraordinary art, particularly in the living room depicting four renowned ancient Greeks, Plato, Aristotle, Sophocles, and Homer, will undoubtedly attract their attention.

Argyros Mansion is open to the public daily, with the exception of Mondays and Thursdays, from May to October, and offers guided tours in both Greek and English for individuals and groups. Furthermore, the mansion's outside spaces are open for special elegant events such as weddings and parties. The opulent exterior transports guests to another period, providing them with a genuinely unique and one-of-a-kind experience.

The Argyros Mansion is one of Santorini's most noteworthy contemporary landmarks, with a great collection of antique furniture and rare paintings and objects dating back to the 19th century.

Santorini's 5 Most Authentic Villages

Isn't it lovely to find a spot where time stops, allowing us to reconnect with our roots and appreciate life's basic joys in an ever-changing world?

If so, Santorini may be the ideal destination for you. It is without a doubt one of the most well-known and popular tourist destinations in the world, offering a magnificent blend of history, culture, and natural beauty.

Although Santorini is well-known for its gorgeous resorts and thrilling nightlife, the island's authentic areas, which have preserved their history and culture and are a true depiction of traditional Greek life, have been concealed behind all the tourist activities.

If you want to get away from the busy tourist areas and experience the island's traditional way of life and timeless charm, consider visiting Akrotiri, Emporio, Mesa Gonia, Pyrgos, and Messaria.

1. Akrotiri - A Hidden Treasure:

Akrotiri is one of Greece's less busy destinations, with beautiful red beaches and historic sites including wonderful ancient ruins.

Akrotiri, located on the island's southwest coast, was one of the most well-known cities and an important economic center. Akrotiri, like Pompeii, was previously destroyed and buried by volcanic ash, but no human remains were discovered. That is why Akrotiri is also known as Greece's Pompeii. However, it has been well maintained, allowing you to enter the world of ancient civilization that can be seen in the Archaeological Museum of Thera.

Akrotiri skillfully mixes history and authenticity with its tiny cobblestone lanes, stone buildings, and tranquil ambiance. Amazing finds such as paintings, ceramics, and household objects can be found here, and you can sense the atmosphere of Akrotiri when it was a thriving and prosperous city.

Despite the fact that much of the island is yet undiscovered and substantial excavation work is ongoing, Akrotiri has several sights that will captivate you. Water cruises, the picturesque Red Beach, the highest point in the village - Venetian Castle and Akrotiri Lighthouse - as well as a secret site called "Pricky Pear" where you can enjoy a spectacular sunset are all available. Aside from that, you can unwind in peace and quiet while dining at one of the village's antique taverns, such as The Good Heart.

2. Emporio - A Journey Through Time

Emporio is a fascinating community with distinct beauty and a rich history that should not be overlooked. It is one of Santorini's largest and oldest settlements, located in the heart of the island. Though it is mostly undiscovered by tourists, it provides a variety of unique experiences.

Emporio features remarkable Cycladic architecture that takes you on a voyage through time. The remains of an ancient stronghold known as Kastelli can be found here - a must-see on Santorini. Kastelli is a maze of hidden tunnels, interesting gardens, vineyards, and underground paths where its people not only built their homes but also churches and chapels.

Emporio will immerse you in the authentic traditional way of life on the island. The churches of St. Nicholas Marmaritis, Old Panaghia, and Metamorfosi Sotiros (Transfiguration) are located here, and they are among the most unique and beautiful in Santorini. The majestic Goulas Tower, an emblem of the island's medieval heritage, is another must-see.

Emporio's history and culture, as well as its warm hospitality and real charm, will enchant you when you visit.

3. Mesa Gonia - A Traditional Time Capsule:

Mesa Gonia is another picturesque village in Santorini's northeast that is well worth a visit. It is the historical hub of the island and one of the most traditional settlements, with old residences and traditions that have been preserved.

Mesa Gonia, also known as Episkopi Gonias, is ideal for a calm holiday away from the tourist throng; nevertheless, the accommodation options are limited.

This small community was previously completely abandoned owing to an earthquake, but residents have begun to return in recent years. The houses have now been renovated and painted, making it a pleasant place to stroll.

The vines and wine of Mesa Gonia are well-known. There are several traditional wineries in the region where you may sample several types of local wine, such as the "Canava Roussos Winery" at the village's entrance. If you are a wine aficionado looking to learn more about the region's rich winemaking history, stop by The Wine Museum, which is conveniently located on the way to Mesa Gonia. This enticing enterprise invites visitors to discover the rich history and skill of winemaking in this charming corner of the world.

The church of Panagia Episkopi, Santorini's oldest church, is one of the primary attractions here. There are also countless little streets worth exploring and photographing.

Mesa Gonia also boasts a plethora of handicraft shops, galleries, and studios where local artisans create stunning ceramics and fabrics. You can buy unique souvenirs and gifts for your loved ones here, creating wonderful memories of your Santorini visit.

4. Pyrgos - Classic Elegance:

Pyrgos is another underappreciated little village whose history may be found in every stone and alley. This tiny village is renowned as one of the most picturesque sites in Santorini, and it is positioned on the island's highest point, providing visitors with breathtaking panoramic views of Greek islands.

Pyrgos was formerly Santorini's capital, and it has retained much of its particular architectural and historical identity. Its snow-white cottages built in the classic

Cycladic architecture, small alleyways, vineyards, and flower gardens create a one-of-a-kind environment that will instantly captivate you.

While Pyrgos is surrounded by the majority of Santorini's vineyards, there is much more to explore. The Pyrgos Castle, the Monastery of Prophet Elias, the church Panagia Eisodia, Aghia Triada, and the Museum of the Past are all historical landmarks that will take you back in time.

There are also cozy taverns and restaurants providing traditional Greek food, such as Kallisti Tavern, where you can enjoy Mediterranean cuisine and local wine while watching the sunrise and sunset away from the crowds of the more touristic towns.

5. Messaria - A Time Travel Adventure:

Messaria is a lovely town surrounded by vineyards. This community is noted for its stylish and classy environment, as well as its neoclassical architecture. While Mesa Gonia has few accommodation options, Messaria has a plethora of hotels, cafes, and restaurants. Messaria has a higher population and busier roadways during the day due to its location on the main route utilized to navigate the island.

Messaria is an excellent destination for wine enthusiasts, as it produces the most wine on the island.

The Argyros Mansion and the Saliveros Mansion are the most well-known tourist attractions in Messaria.

Messaria's distinct allure is visible in the evening, when the streets are lighted with lanterns and people gather for walks and amusement. Here, you may feel the warmth and compassion of the Greek people while taking in the atmosphere of a truly traditional village.

Santorini has a lot more to offer than its Instagram-famous spots. Each of Santorini's towns - Akrotiri, Emporio, Mesa Gonia, Pyrgos, and Messaria - will allow you to escape the rush and bustle of daily life and appreciate Santorini's authentic beauty away from the crowds.

Chapter 19: Engaging in Watersports Activities in Santorini

Because Santorini is a renowned tourist destination, there are numerous clubs that offer watersports. They can be found in the island's most popular beaches (Kamari, Perissa, Perivolos), but also in Oia. Visitors can enjoy a wonderful day at the beach by participating in a variety of water games and other activities. The watersports offered range from jet skis and runner boats to stand up paddle boards. Learn more

Let's have a look at the numerous Santorini Watersports available one by one:
Jetski Safari
Jetski safari is an adventure of a lifetime that should not be missed at any cost. Among the available watersports, that fascinating recreational activity is a hidden gem. There are normally two regular trips to fall in love with Santorini's black beaches and turquoise waters - one around the south coast and the other around the volcano. Before finishing the tour, one can relax by snorkeling and visiting the beaches along the way.

If you enjoy speed on the water, this is the sport for you. Feel the engine buzz as you sail along the shores of Santorini at full speed, appreciating the island's beauty from the water. You can go around the islands or take a short excursion to the famed volcano and National Natural Geological Park of Nea Kameni. The departure point is usually the most beautiful beach on Santorini, St George, followed by Vlychada and the red beach for your jet-ski adventure. Whether you go solo or with companions, it's a great way to appreciate the scenery while getting a few thrills in the process.

Jet skiing for 30 minutes in Santorini costs between 40 and 50 euros, depending on the instructor. You may, however, schedule a jet skiing adventure for up to 4 hours, which will cost you between 220 and 250 euros. You'll be relieved to learn that no prior expertise is required to go jet skiing, and that with a standard training session, you'll be ready to tackle the deep waters.

Sea Kayaking

The relaxing sensation of gliding through water in a kayak is not restricted to lakes. Santorini also has opportunities for water kayaking. Around Perivolos beach, there are numerous groups offering guided kayaking tours or kayak rentals. Viewing the exciting caldera and volcano whilst on the expedition is a tremendous plus. After kayaking to the southern coast, guests can go snorkeling and swimming in Santorini's azure waters.

Seakayaking in Santorini is an unforgettable way to explore the island's coastline. With this guided tour along the south coast, you can see the caldera and volcano from a different perspective while admiring the landscape of whitewashed houses and rock formations during the day, or you can wait until the evening to see the sunset with its sublime red color on the surface of the sea. With a quick beginning lesson teaching you how to paddle effortlessly, you can row around the south shore and enjoy swimming and diving in Santorini's crystal-clear seas in no time. In perspective, this is a lovely program.

Flyboarding

Flyboarding is an extreme watersport that is becoming increasingly popular among visitors. Flying, jumping, and diving in and out of the sea's chilly blue water is an exhilarating and must-do activity when visiting Santorini. Flyboarding, with its freestyle movements and freedom, provides the rider with a unique and distinctive sensation, which is complemented by the spectacular views of the beaches.

Wakeboard

Wakeboarding is one of the more exciting and modern watersports activities accessible for fun at Kamari Beach. This rewarding hobby can fill you with joy in the early mornings when there are no winds and the lake is peaceful. The activity is addictive, and hiring certified professionals to train you takes little time.

Parasailing

Gliding over the water in a parachute attached to a boat while taking in the beauty of Perivolos Beach is a thrilling experience. Everything is unforgettable when seen from a height of 300 feet above the lake. And if it's the sunset you're after, nights are the greatest time to go, making the whole thing a satisfying thrill with a lovely backdrop.

If you're seeking for an extra rush to get your pulse racing, it's time to take to the skies and see Santorini from a fresh angle. You will securely fly over the beautiful seas of the Aegean Sea with a panoramic view of Santorini from 100 meters up, capture photos from the skies, and, if you're lucky, enjoy a front row seat to a spectacular sunset if you go parasailing in Santorini. The parachute can hold up to three people and is towed by a specially built rigger, so strap in and quickly glide around this lovely island in style.

Crazy Squab

When traveling in a group, crazy squab is a perfectly tailored recreational activity among the many watersports. Riding the harsh waves tethered to harnesses on an inflatable sofa in the middle of the sea is a unique experience one can have when visiting Santorini.

The Greek island of Santorini is a wonderful option for a journey full with thrills and breathtaking scenery. The stunning sunsets and views of the volcanic islands and beaches are just the icing on the cake. Santorini Watersports is something that all tourists should do in order to fully experience the glories of the water and the island's beauty. There is a lot to do and admire here, from extreme watersports to wave-riding sports to simple canoeing.

SUP (Stand Up Paddleboarding)

If you're a seasoned surfer seeking for large waves and barrels, keep rolling, but if you want to appreciate the Aegean Sea's serene and glassy surface on a board, consider a SUP session. Discover a totally unique way to enjoy the jaw-dropping views of the islands while getting in an all-over body exercise as you sail on Santorini's modest waves standing on a board, using just pure man-power and a paddle to lead you. Santorini is known for its small paradise beaches, but Saint George's beach is one of the widest, making it the ideal place to relax and paddle around in the flat water, and there are also yoga lessons on the paddle boards if you feel like it. SUP in Santorini is the perfect activity to put your balance and paddle power to the test, and it's really amazing if you catch one of the spectacular sunsets in the villages of Oia, Fira, and Imerovigli.

Scuba diving

Scuba diving is one of the world's most popular adventure sports. Scuba diving in Santorini is regarded as the sport's Mecca for various reasons. The stunning blue waters are the main reason visitors come to Santorini to explore the deep end.

Diving choices vary depending on your skill level. Santorini has it everything, from beginner's lessons to advanced PADI courses. All you have to worry about before the courses is your ability to be comfortable in water and know what you're getting yourself into. Caldera Beach is home to one of the most unusual geological formations on the planet. Explore the active volcano over the caldera reef and unique cave systems, as well as the technicolor macro life, stunning swim-throughs, and hot springs!

Except for the cold months of November and February, you may go scuba diving in Santorini all year. Please click the following link to view all of our scuba diving activities in Santorini.

Sailing

It's time to get your sea legs - there's no better way to view a Santorini sunset than by sailing in Santorini and cruise over the Aegean Sea! As the climax of your voyage around the volcano island, sail just below the caldera, then sit back and relax with a drink while taking in the scenery. This sailboat or catamaran trip is not the most extreme of our options, but it is by far the most pleasant. The hot springs are the first stop for a mud bath, which is a unique and therapeutic method to relax. Then, via Apronisi and the village's iconic lighthouse, you'll make a second stop at the red beach to swim and dive in Santorini's beautiful waters. You will continue going to White Beach to swim and have a BBQ, and after supper, you will sail gently to the village of Oia to enjoy the sunset with its unique gradations of pink, purple, orange, and red.

Snorkeling

The depths of water reached by participants are the primary distinction between snorkeling and scuba diving. While scuba diving involves diving to significant depths in the water, snorkeling is normally done near the surface. Snorkeling equipment is less sophisticated than that used for scuba diving.

We couldn't discuss about top outdoor activities in Sanorini without mentioning snorkeling in Satorini. It's practically a crime to visit Santorini and not discover its stunning pale blue waters! An activity that lasts about 100 minutes might take you to Perivolos, where you can experience the volcanic surroundings.

A trip for two people will cost roughly 300 euros, but anyone after that will have to pay around 75 euros per person. If you want to go Snorkeling in Santorini, then follow the link provided.

Chapter 20: Santorini Snorkeling Guide - Top 10 Spots, Ideal Time, and More

Many people are unaware that Santorini is an excellent snorkeling destination. This island's renown is limited to panoramic beaches with breathtaking ocean vistas. When you go snorkeling in Santorini, however, you will have the opportunity to uncover the best resources. Santorini, while not as rich in marine life as other Greek islands such as Corfu, is nevertheless a wonderful destination for diving in the crystalline waters to explore the fascinating undersea rocky formations. This island has various attractions such as caves, shipwrecks, and more, making it an excellent snorkeling spot.

Santorini's water is crystal clear. It has good visibility, which means that people can go as far as they wish. On this island, you can see down to 40 meters underwater. You may explore the magnificent reefs and see the colorful fish species. Mold currents have the best coral reef formations, and various fish and invertebrates prefer their stay in these waters.

1. Caldera Beach

Caldera Beach is also known as Balos. The best diving place in Santorini is on a black sandy beach. It gets its name from the fact that it is the only beach in the

Caldera, or volcanic crater, that does not require transportation by boat. Visitors can simply get here. You only need to travel towards Akrotiri and then turn right at the Caldera sign. Surprisingly, Caldera Beach is also an excellent snorkeling location on this remote island. It lacks the hectic tourist environment of Santorini's other famed beaches. Deep waters with a plethora of fish can be found here.

2. Kokini Paralia (Red Beach)

Red Beach is a popular tourist spot in Santorini known for its red-hued sand caused by the presence of frozen lava. It is not just one of the most famous beaches on the island, but it is also an excellent snorkeling area. With its stunning landscape of volcanic rocks, red cliffs, and the namesake red sand, this beach provides a wonderful experience. The sea here is so quiet that you may snorkel and see the fascinating underwater caverns and rocks. Rentable umbrellas and sunbeds are available.

The Red Beach is near Akrotiri in the southern section of Santorini. Visitors can get there by boat from Akrotiri, Perissa, or Kamari. You can also approach the Red Beach parking lot by land by following the road that leads to the ancient Akrotiri Town archeological site. Furthermore, keep in mind that this beach is relatively tiny and gets packed rapidly. To avoid crowds, you must arrive early in the morning.

3. Aspri Paralia's White Beach

White Beach, located on the southwest shore near Akrotiri, is another appealing snorkeling location in Santorini. It is famous for its gleaming white cliffs, dark volcanic sand, and crystal clear seas. White Beach is an excellent snorkeling location where you may explore various caverns underwater. White Beach is only accessible by boat from the beaches of Perissa and Akrotiri. This beach is far less crowded than Red Beach. However, because it is a small cove, it can get busy during high season. Arrive early in the morning if you want to enjoy peace while swimming on this beach.

4. Kamari Beach is number four.

Kamari is one of Santorini's busiest resort villages. It is a family-friendly island destination where people of all ages may enjoy a relaxing yet action-packed holiday. Kamari Beach is a black pebbly beach with crystal clear water that allows you to readily watch marine life underwater. During the day, you may relax by the sea on the 2 km long fully organized beach, which offers a variety of amenities such as water sports and sunbed rental. In the evening, there are numerous places to dine and drink along the main walkway.

Mesa Vouno mountain separates Kamari and Perissa beaches. The Ancient Thera is a historical landmark located on the summit of this mountain. It is also a must-see attraction in Santorini for history and archeology buffs, with breathtaking vistas. In addition, the black volcanic sand on this beach gets particularly hot in the summer, so bring your swimming shoes.

5. Perissa Beach

Perissa Beach is one of Santorini's most well-known. Notably, while having a long and large area, it is not as congested as the popular Oia or Fira beaches. Perissa is an easily accessible resort area on Santorini's southeast coast, located at the base of the Mesa Vouno Mountain. Perissa is a Blue Flag beach because of its cleanliness and pure waters.

Those looking for a clean, shallow, kid-friendly beach in Santorini can go to Perissa Beach. The sea bed here is made up of black sand and small volcanic pebbles. This beach has warmer water. While snorkeling, you can see Mediterranean fish species as well as crabs and starfish. Aside from it, there are a variety of services accessible, such as beach equipment rental, a playground, a water park with slides, and water sports such as windsurfing and canoeing. There are also numerous restaurants and bars near Perissa Beach. All of these factors combine to make it a worthy destination.

6. Ammoudi Beach

Ammoudi Beach is one of the most beautiful beaches in Santorini. It is located on the northwest shore of the island, near the Ammoudi harbor in the bottom of Oia. Notably, this is not your typical sandy beach for sunbathing on a lounge chair, but rather a cove that is a fantastic site for swimming and snorkeling in Santorini. The water here is a deep blue color with crystal-clear visibility, tempting you to jump in.

If you want to swim, you can get into the sea right away from the small dock, but if you want to dive, you must take the trail over the restaurants that leads to a small bay. It is bordered by steep red cliffs. In addition, there is a small islet here known as St. Nicholas Rock, which has a small church. Visitors can only get there by swimming.

7. Vlychada Beach (Paralia Vlichada)

Vlychada Beach is not a busy tourist destination like other renowned spots in Santorini's south, yet it is one of the most picturesque. Many people are unaware of this beach. The wind-shaped cliffs that encircle the regions and seem like sand sculptures are the most notable feature of this beach. These cliffs give this beach the appearance of a lunar landscape, which is why it is also known as Moon Beach.

Along with the beautiful environment, this spot boasts clear and somewhat deep waters with a variety of fish, making Vlychada beach an excellent snorkeling location in Santorini. There are also adjacent snack cafes and taverns to make your stay more comfortable.

8. Kambia Beach

The next stop on our agenda is Kambia, a less well-known destination on the southwest coast between the famous Red and White beaches. There is no direct route to this place, and the only approach to Kambia is by a dirt road. Notable features include a tiny pub and sunbed rentals. However, there are no opulent bars or restaurants, which is why this location is less well-known and isolated.

Surprisingly, this tranquil beach attracts guests who prefer to spend their vacations alone, away from the crowded tourist beaches. The seafloor here is littered with huge pebbles, making walking along the beach slightly difficult. It is recommended that you wear water shoes. There is a little wooden wharf with a staircase that allows easy access to the water. The clean waters are ideal for snorkeling and seeing numerous species, sea urchins, and even octopuses among the rocks.

9. Nea Kameni

Nea Kameni is a small island located in the caldera of Santorini. Notably, it is a magnificent area that has become famous due to the presence of a sunken shipwreck on this site for decades. Nea Kameni has become one of the most well-known snorkeling and scuba diving destinations. Visitors can also explore the area around this beach. You can visit the natural hot springs and the island's western area, which is a must-see.

The water on this island is incredibly pure and clear, and you can easily see up to 40 feet underwater. During the summer, when the water is roiled by northerly breezes, the surrounding rocks might become a concern. However, most of the year, this location is clear for snorkeling.

10. Black Beach

The Black Beach is one of the rockiest coves on Santorini's southern coast. Because of its unusual location, it is the least popular beach on the island. The beach is located beneath the orthodox chapel, where the accessible path terminates. The shoreline is sandier and rougher, and as a result, the area experiences roily water. This beach's water may not be suited for swimming. Still, it's worth a shot.

Because there aren't many people in this area, it appeals to snorkelers. Surprisingly, the best spot of this beach for snorkeling is at the easternmost end of its shoreline. There are caves and rock shelters all throughout the area that are home to colorful fish and sea urchins. A big white stone wedge emerges from the ocean. The cliffs also illustrate ancient Greek folklore.

When is the best time to snorkel in Santorini?

The peak season in Santorini is thought to be the best time to go snorkeling on the island. Summer months, from June to September, are the busiest for tourists. During this season, the most flights are available. Early morning hikes and water bathing are very popular at this time of year. The sun is shining brightly, the glistening waters are enticing, the winds are gentle, and the air is clean. This season, Santorini has the most wonderful beach weather. As a result, it is an excellent time to go swimming, scuba diving, or snorkeling in the waters.

How to Reserve a Snorkeling Tour in Santorini

Santorini activities can be booked through online tour and adventure activity platforms or through local operators. In Santorini, many travel and adventure activity businesses offer snorkeling excursions. You are free to use any platform of your choice. Simply go to their website, which allows for easy searching and speedy booking of snorkeling in Santorini packages. Several local providers, such as Caldera Beach, which offers diving and snorkeling tours in Santorini, are also available at the activity spots. They provide guided snorkeling tours, cruise vacations, and other services.

Snorkeling Tips

- When snorkeling for the first time, try starting from the shore rather than a boat. It is because jumping from a boat into the deep sea might be difficult for beginners.
- Choose to snorkel from an area of the beach that is alive, i.e., has a variety of fish and coral reefs to see, for an unforgettable experience. It will be more fun than snorkeling in a barren area with little to see.
- Most of the time, waves diminish underwater visibility, making it difficult to see aquatic life. As a result, novice snorkelers should enter the water when it is calm.
- When you're new to snorkeling, watching other snorkelers in the water helps you feel more at ease. This gives you an idea of the circumstances underwater.
- Always go snorkeling on a beach with a lifeguard as a precaution. You can also go with an experienced snorkeler if you like.
- Remember that snorkeling restricts your breathing. As a result, you must maintain your activity level reasonable so that you do not have to breathe heavily.
- Use no harmful sunscreen. Most sunscreens are known to harm coral reefs. So, use a reef-safe sunscreen that will not harm marine life.

All of the snorkeling guidelines listed above are about taking care of oneself. You should also respect the sea by not touching the coral reefs, fish species, or other organisms in it. Furthermore, you should not bring any valuable stuff with you to avoid loss.

Chapter 21: Culinary Exploration in Santorini: A Gastronomic Tour of Premier Restaurants

Santorini, a beautiful Greek island in the Aegean Sea, is famous not only for its spectacular sunsets and attractive blue-domed houses, but also for its wonderful culinary scene.

The island is home to a myriad of restaurants that serve a wide variety of cuisine that combine traditional Greek flavors with modern culinary skills. Santorini's eating options cater to every appetite, from seaside tavernas with spectacular views to quiet cafes nestled away in narrow alleys. Here's a detailed list of some of the greatest eateries on this magical island.

Ammoudi Fish Taverna: Nestled at the base of Oia's renowned cliffs, Ammoudi Fish Taverna provides a traditional Greek eating experience. This seaside taverna, known for its fresh seafood, allows guests to relish the catch of the day while enjoying unobstructed views of the caldera. The grilled octopus and lobster pasta are outstanding items, and the warm and pleasant service complements them.

Fira - Argo Restaurant: Argo Restaurant, located in the heart of Fira, is known for its classic Greek food with a modern twist. The spacious patio overlooks the caldera, creating an enchanting setting for a romantic evening. The cuisine includes mezze, moussaka, and exquisite lamb dishes. Don't pass up the chance to combine your meal with a glass of Assyrtiko wine from the region.

To Psaraki in Akrotiri is a hidden gem for a taste of real Greek cuisine away from the crowded tourist districts. The beachfront restaurant specializes on seafood, and the grilled sardines and calamari are highly recommended. The tranquil atmosphere is created by the rustic surroundings and the sound of the waves.

Pyrgos - Selene Restaurant: Selene Restaurant is a gastronomic institution on the island, located in the medieval village of Pyrgos. The restaurant is well-known for its devotion to using local, organic ingredients, and it offers a gastronomic trip through the flavors of Santorini. Diners can enjoy a variety of inventive meals coupled with great Greek wines on the tasting menu.

To Pinakio: If you happen to be on Kamari's black sand beach, To Pinakio is a beautiful taverna that encapsulates the essence of Greek hospitality. This family-run restaurant offers a relaxing ambiance and a good choice for a leisurely lunch by the sea, with a menu offering grilled meats, moussaka, and fresh salads.

Tranquilo in Perissa: Tranquilo in Perissa offers a relaxed and modern dining experience. This seaside restaurant and cocktail bar combines Greek and international flavors, with a menu that includes sushi, burgers, and inventive cocktails. The lively atmosphere and live music make it a favorite of both locals and visitors.

Megalochori - Raki: Raki is a classic taverna in the scenic town of Megalochori famed for its homestyle Greek meals. The warm ambiance and pleasant service give the impression that you are dining in a local's home. The moussaka and souvlaki are popular dishes, and the large wine selection features the best of Santorini's vineyards.

Vanilia in Firostefani is a popular choice for couples looking for a memorable dining experience, thanks to its romantic atmosphere and lighted tables. The menu combines Greek and Mediterranean cuisine, with a focus on fresh, seasonal ingredients. The sea bass and prawn linguine are particularly delicious, and the vast wine list compliments the varied meal.

Exo Gonia - Metaxi Mas: For a genuinely authentic experience, travel to Exo Gonia and discover Metaxi Mas. This taverna, housed in a historic building, emanates charm and provides classic Greek cuisine served with a homemade touch. The grilled meats, packed vine leaves, and local wine choices make it a local and tourist favorite.

To summarize, Santorini's food culture is as varied and enthralling as its landscapes. Whether you enjoy dining by the sea, on a cliffside terrace, or in a lovely village, the island has something for everyone. Santorini's eateries guarantee a fascinating voyage through the flavors of the Mediterranean, from traditional Greek tavernas to sophisticated restaurants displaying modern gastronomy. So, appreciate the wines, indulge in the local cuisine, and allow the beauty of Santorini's dining experiences enrich your amazing island holiday.

Chapter 22: Exploring Local Cuisine in Santorini

Santorini cuisine and Santorini Local Food are distinguished by dishes including elements inextricably tied to the Mediterranean diet. Because of the volcanic soil, the island's agricultural industry offers unique culinary delights, satisfying even the most discerning palates.

You will most likely be hungry when you get in Santorini. If you're wondering what tastes to try, we've compiled a list of classic local foods to eat during your stay in Santorini that will take you away from the norm.

Santorini is also a flavor pioneer, demonstrating the richness and variety of the Greek islands' wonderful native goods.

Rent a car by picking the sort of car you want, at the Santorini location you choose, at the price that only Santorini Holiday Cars can promise, and visit the many Santorini restaurants and bars to sample the great local delicacies!

Fava Santorini

Along with great local wines, tomatoes, and native capers, Fava Santorini is one of the most essential items on the island and Santorini's Local Food. The fava is derived from lathurus clymenum, a native type of yellow peas (not to be confused with beans). The exploitation of the fava has been steadily and solely established on the island for more than 3,500 years, according to Bronze Age archaeological findings.

Fava Santorini is the basic dish for the islanders, eaten in a variety of ways depending on the season.

The summer dish is called "pantremeni (married)" and is cooked with red tomato sauce. During the winter, fava is served with fried crab (smoked pork).

Santorini tomatokeftedes (pseudokeftedes)

One of the most popular appetizers in Santorini is tomato keftedes (or pseudokeftedes as it is known on the island), which is made with Santorini tomatoes, basil, and mint.

The island's famous tomato keftedes, made from Santorinian tomatoes, have a distinct aroma and flavor that will whet your appetite before the main course.

Today, Santorini tomato is one of the island's signature products, and there is a pate factory that gives reason to believe that the native tomato type will continue to create a variety of products.

Kopania

If you're looking for inspiration in a place's traditional local food, Kopania demands your attention. They are typically fashioned in the shape of tiny rolls of barley, raisins, and sesame seeds. It is a really simple-tasting dessert that is both healthy and nutritious. Kopania is the answer if you want to consume something sweet yet avoid fat. Kopania is regarded one of Santorini's most traditional desserts in Santorini Local Food and comes in a variety of flavors, including wine.

Melitinia

Melitinia is a sweet dessert served at numerous celebrations and weddings on the Greek island of Santorini. They're created with salted mizithra and yogurt that's been seasoned with mastic. They may be found at Santorini's traditional bakeries, and they are quite similar to the durtuletia, which are also made and served during feasts and weddings.

Carpaccio Apochti

Apochti is a type of pork that has been baked with salt, vinegar, cinnamon, chopped parsley, and black pepper. It takes at least four days to create because the spices must be sun-dried, but once finished, it may be eaten several days later - either sliced or used in other dishes. Apochti has Byzantine origins, as demonstrated by the name "apochti" (the Byzantine term for this gourmet treat is apoktin).

Chlorotyri (Chloro Tyri)

The traditional Santorini cheese is called "Chlorotyri" and is made from goat or sheep milk. It's creamy and somewhat sour, and if you find it in Santorini, try it! Produced in limited amounts by local makers, making it tough to find!

It is a highly limited-production local cheese that you can not get anywhere else in Greece. Chlorotyri is spread on bread or put into salads.

Santorini Tomatoes

Santorini is recognized not just for its natural beauty, but also for its distinctive tomatoes. Santorini tomatoes are so little that most visitors to the island don't believe they're real. The volcanic soil of the island helps to the creation of Santorini's tomatoes, which are unique and grown uniquely on the island. It is a rich crimson color with a rough exterior that contrasts with a luscious interior.

Small trenches 30cm apart are formed on the ground for traditional tomato production, where numerous dried seeds are placed. Sowing occurs in February, and harvesting occurs from late June to early August. The harvest season is a time of great celebration on the Greek island of Santorini.

Santorini White Eggplant

White eggplant is another unique Santorini Local Food with several comparative advantages. It has few seeds, absorbs little oil when fried, and has a notably sweet flavor. White eggplant may be found in a variety of eateries on the island and is well worth tasting, but we recommend the eggplant salad with white aubergines. It is the ideal complement to ouzo or wine.

Santorini Wines

Santorini wines include Asyrtiko, Athiri, Aidani, Mandilaria, and Mavrotragano. Santorini is a wine-producing island. The island has been producing wine since antiquity, but under the influence of the Venetians throughout the Middle Ages, Santorini wine became world-famous. The contemporary vinification of Santorini retains an Italian influence: the most famous sweet wine of Tuscany is called Vin Santo. Santorini Vin Santo ("Vinsanto" to distinguish it from Tuscan wine) is prepared from grapes that have been sun-dried after harvest.

Many wineries can be found in Santorini, which is a Greek equivalent of Napa Valley, where you can watch the production process and sample various local wines. Santorini is one of the most gorgeous destinations on the planet. Santorini has roughly forty domestic grape varietals, and the vines are low to protect from high winds. The unusual character of Santorini wine is primarily due to the island's unique volcanic terrain.

Skordomakarona

Skordomakarona is made with pasta, fresh Santorini tomatoes, olive oil, garlic, and salt. A delicious and flavorful dish!

Glyko Koufeto

"Koufeto" is the most famous traditional sweet in Santorini, and it is still offered at weddings and festivals today, but it is also widely available in the island's Local Food shops.

Taste these fantastic tiny sweets created by the Union of Santorini Cooperatives with your coffee, cake, and even ice cream as part of a beautiful and tasty wedding ceremony in Santorini and throughout Greece!

The only ingredients in "Koufeto" are honey and almonds. These elements are thought to represent the couple's future. Honey represents a sweet life, while almonds represent fertility.

Kardamydes

Kardamydes are fantastic green herbs that work miracles in the fight against cholesterol. They are collected in farms and vineyards throughout Santorini at the end of April. During this season, they are also available in Fira's central market and several Santorini Local Food shops. They are a fantastic addition to fish food, and because they are difficult to find, try them wherever you find them!

Santorini Cucumber "Katsuni"

The cucumbers growing on Santorini are known as Katsuni by the locals. It is larger than a regular cucumber, with thicker skin and more seeds. If not picked up quickly, it turns sweet and has a melon flavor! Katsuni is unique to Santorini because it can only be found there. It has a milder, colder flavor than normal cucumbers and is a staple in local salads.

The Ultimate Santorini Food Guide [2024] Santorini Restaurants

Santorini is famous not only for its breathtaking sunsets and scenic landscapes, but also for its great food scene. The island offers a unique blend of traditional

Greek cuisine with a modern twist thanks to its vast selection of locally obtained ingredients. The island is well-known for its fresh fish, homegrown vegetables, and distinctive white eggplants. Furthermore, Santorini has a rich wine culture, including some of Greece's most known wineries. Overall, the dining scene on the island has something for everyone.

Tipping in Greece: If you're planning a trip to Santorini, knowing that tipping is common in Greece will come in handy. A reasonable rule of thumb for a casual dinner at a taverna is to leave a gratuity of about €2 to €5, or round up your amount to the nearest €0 or €5. For example, if your bill is €46, you could leave €50. Higher-end restaurants expect a 5 to 10% gratuity, with 15% considered generous. When ordering at a bar or café, rounding up to the nearest euro is welcomed. For table service, a gratuity of 5 to 10% is recommended.

Restaurant Reservations: It is best to book reservations in advance for the restaurants listed below to ensure a pleasant dining experience. Typically, getting a table 3 to 5 days in advance is sufficient, but for special occasions, booking a table weeks, or even months, in advance is recommended to ensure availability.

Food is an important aspect of many travelers' vacation experiences. Nothing beats a wonderful lunch at a top-rated restaurant after a day of seeing the island's stunning beaches and historic attractions. Santorini boasts an abundance of excellent dining options, making it an ideal visit for foodies.

Santorini is famed for several delectable delicacies, the most famous of which are arguably "ntomatokeftedes," or tomato fritters. These are created with Santorini tomatoes produced locally, combined with herbs and flour, then deep-fried till crispy. They make an excellent beginning or light meal, especially when paired with a glass of local white wine.

How to Select a Santorini Restaurant

When looking for the top restaurants in Santorini, there are various variables to consider. The restaurant's location is an important consideration. Some restaurants provide spectacular views of the island's caldera, while others are in charming villages or along the beach.

A restaurant's ambiance and decor can also influence the dining experience. Some restaurants have sophisticated, premium decor, but others have a more informal, laid-back atmosphere.

Of course, the most important factor is the food's quality. Santorini is famous for its fresh, local ingredients and traditional Greek food. From seafood to meat dishes and vegetarian options, there is something for everyone.

It should be noted that dining out in Santorini can be pricey, particularly in major tourist regions. However, there are many affordable solutions available, particularly in smaller communities away from the big tourist destinations.

Finally, customer reviews can provide useful information about the quality of a restaurant. Online review services such as TripAdvisor and Yelp might assist in locating the top restaurants in Santorini.

But... Is eating out in Santorini expensive?

To address your question, dining out in Santorini, particularly in famous tourist areas, can be pricey. However, there are many inexpensive solutions available, particularly in rural communities away from the big tourist destinations.

Santorini's Best Restaurants

When it comes to dining, Santorini has a wealth of possibilities. The island has it all, from high-end restaurants to street food to foreign cuisine to traditional tavernas. We've compiled a list of our favorite eateries in various Santorini locales.

Oia Restaurants Santorini

Oia is a lovely hamlet on Santorini's northern point, noted for its breathtaking sunsets and stunning caldera vistas. Here are some of the best restaurants in Oia to visit:

Restaurant Roka | Oia

Roka is a modern Greek restaurant in the center of Oia. The modern decor and attractive outdoor dining area of the restaurant create a fashionable and romantic setting, ideal for a memorable night out. The menu includes inventive takes on traditional Greek foods, such as tomato fritters and grilled squid with black garlic aioli. The wine list is very vast, with both domestic and international alternatives. Roka's prices are on the higher side, but the quality of the meal and the environment make it well worth the extra money.
P: +30 2286 071896

Ammoudi Fish Tavern

Ammoudi Fish Tavern is a picturesque coastal restaurant in Ammoudi, a little fishing community just below Oia. With tables positioned directly on the water's edge and a spectacular sunset view, the restaurant provides a unique dining experience. The menu emphasizes fresh seafood, with daily catches displayed on ice for diners to enjoy. The grilled octopus and lobster spaghetti are two of the most popular dishes. Ammoudi Fish Tavern's prices are on the pricier side, but the incomparable setting and cuisine quality make it a must-visit restaurant in Santorini.
P: +30 2286 072298

Oia's Karma Restaurant

Karma is a modern and stylish Santorini restaurant. Located in the middle of Oia, with stunning views of the caldera. The restaurant's design mixes modern with classic Greek characteristics, creating a one-of-a-kind dining experience.

The menu at Karma focuses on Mediterranean and Asian fusion cuisine, with an emphasis on fresh, locally produced ingredients. There are also vegetarian and gluten-free alternatives on the menu. Thai green curry, grilled fish with quinoa salad, and lamb chops with aubergine puree are among the signature meals.

Karma's prices are on the higher side, but the food and service are worth it. Reservations are strongly advised, especially during peak season.

P: +30 2286 071404

Fira Restaurants

Argo Restaurant | Fira

Argo is one of Fira's most famous restaurants, situated on a cliffside with breathtaking views of the Aegean Sea. Traditional Greek cuisine is served at the restaurant, which uses fresh and local products. Argo provides a charming and intimate setting, ideal for a special occasion or a romantic supper.

Grilled octopus, fava bean dip, and lamb chops are among the specialty meals. Their wine list is particularly outstanding, showcasing some of the top Santorini and Greek wines.

Argo's prices are on the higher side, with appetizers starting at €16 and main dishes ranging from €28 to €48.

Argo's food, service, and ambiance have all gotten rave reviews from customers. Customers rave about the restaurant's spectacular vistas, superb culinary quality, and excellent service.

P: +30 2286 022594

The Ftelos Brewery

Ftelos Brewery, located in Fira, is a hidden gem famed for its specialty brews and superb pub-style meals. The restaurant features a relaxed and pleasant ambiance, with both indoor and outdoor dining.

Ftelos Brewery's specialty meals include burgers, fish & chips, and chicken wings. The brewery also serves a wide range of local and foreign artisan beers.

The menu at Ftelos Brewery is reasonably priced, with appetizers starting at €6 and main dishes ranging from €10 to €16.

Customers enjoy the brewery's casual and welcoming atmosphere, as well as the high quality of its cuisine and beer. The service is likewise highly regarded, with employees going above and above to make their guests feel at ease.

P: +30 2286 186627

Ouzeri

Ouzeri is a typical Greek taverna in Fira's core, serving classic Greek cuisine in a casual and pleasant setting. The restaurant features an inviting atmosphere and both indoor and outdoor dining.

Moussaka, filled vine leaves, and grilled fish are among the specialty meals at Ouzeri. In addition, the restaurant has a large collection of Greek wines and spirits.

The menu at Ouzeri is reasonably priced, with appetizers starting at €8 and main meals ranging from €12 to €22.

Ouzeri has earned rave reviews from customers who praised the restaurant's superb food, courteous service, and outstanding value for money.

P: +30 2286 021566

Candouni | Pyrgos

Candouni is a charming family-run restaurant in the heart of Pyrgos village on Santorini. The restaurant has a lovely outside seating area with spectacular views of Santorini's caldera.

The menu combines traditional Greek and Mediterranean dishes with fresh, locally produced ingredients. Lamb kleftiko, grilled octopus, and handmade moussaka are all must-order meals.

Candouni is an excellent alternative for people looking for a genuine dining experience because the prices are cheap for the quality of food and setting.

P: +30 2286 071616

Anogi | Pyrgos

Anogi is a quaint family-run taverna in Pyrgos' old hamlet, away from the tourist hordes. The menu features classic Greek food with a modern touch, prepared using fresh local ingredients. The ambiance is cozy and peaceful, with a stunning view of the island.

Pork tenderloin with quince, fava dip, tomato keftedes, and handmade pastries are among the signature dishes. They also provide a large selection of local wines to complement your meal.

The pricing range is reasonable, with most dishes costing between 10 and 20 euros.

Anogi has gotten rave reviews from customers, with many appreciating the food's quality, the pleasant service, and the tranquil atmosphere.

P: +30 2286 021285

To Psaraki | Vlychada

To Psaraki is a seafood restaurant in Vlychada, Greece, known for its fresh fish and seafood dishes. The restaurant is located on the beach and offers breathtaking views of the sea and nearby cliffs.

Grilled octopus, seafood spaghetti, and fried calamari are among the signature meals. They also have a large selection of Greek wines to go with your meal.

The prices range from moderate to high, with most dishes costing between 20 and 40 euros.

To Psaraki has gotten rave reviews from customers, with many appreciating the food's quality, the lovely location, and the attentive service.

P: +30 2286 082783

Food Tours in Santorini

Gourmet meal tour and wine tasting in Santorini: Discover the best of Santorini with a gourmet food tour and wine tasting. Begin your journey by visiting a classic winery. Discover the finest ingredients on the island and learn how to prepare wonderful dishes with a professional chef.

Walking Food Tour in Santorini: Looking for a different way to spend your morning in Santorini? Then come along with us on our Santorini walking food tour! This relaxed walking tour takes you through some of the most gorgeous sections of the island while also enabling you to enjoy some of the great native delicacies and beverages.

Santorini Wine Tour: A Santorini wine tour is the ideal way to experience everything this magnificent location has to offer. You'll have intriguing chats about winemaking processes and the unique procedure employed in Santorini, and you'll learn everything there is to know about viticulture on the island.

Restaurant Dining Tips in Santorini

When planning a trip to Santorini, one of the joys of the experience is dining out. Here are some pointers to help you make the most of your culinary adventure:

- Making reservations: It is strongly advised to make reservations in advance, particularly during peak season. Some of the top restaurants in Santorini fill up quickly, so it's important to book ahead of time.
- Dress code: While formal attire is not needed, certain restaurants have a smart-casual dress code. To minimize surprises, always verify the dress code on the restaurant's website or give them a call.
- Tipping customs: Tipping is common but not required in Santorini. A regular 10% tip is usually sufficient, but if you experienced exceptional service, feel free to offer more.
- Trying local specialties: Santorini is well-known for its traditional dishes such as fava, tomatokeftedes, and white eggplant salad. During your visit, don't be afraid to try these regional dishes and explore new flavors.

Exploring Santorini's off-the-beaten-path restaurants

While the most prominent restaurants in Santorini are frequently found in Oia and Fira, there are many hidden treasures worth discovering. Request tips from locals or wander off the main path to find new dining experiences.

Here are some answers to frequently asked questions about dining in Santorini restaurants:

How much does a lunch cost on Santorini, Greece?

For a mid-range restaurant, the typical cost of a meal in Santorini is around €20-30 per person.

When is supper in Santorini?

Dinner in Santorini is usually served between 7:00 and 11:00 p.m.

Is tipping usual in Santorini? In Santorini, how much do you tip?

Tipping is traditional in Santorini, and a 10% gratuity is usually adequate.

Are bookings required in Santorini?

Is it necessary to make reservations for restaurants in Santorini in advance? It is strongly advised to book reservations in advance, particularly during peak season.

Should I pay with cash or a credit card in Santorini?

Although both cash and credit cards are generally accepted in Santorini, it's always a good idea to have some cash on hand for minor transactions and in case of any problems with card payments.

Santorini is a foodie's heaven, with a variety of eateries serving up superb cuisine and stunning vistas. In this chapter, we've highlighted some of the best places to dine on the island, from traditional tavernas to modern gourmet restaurants. We strongly advise you to dine at these establishments during your vacation to Santorini. There is something for everyone, whether you want fresh fish, local specialties, or inventive cuisine.

When dining in Santorini, variables such as location, ambiance, food, and price range must all be considered. We recommend making reservations in advance, especially during high season, and dressing appropriately. Try some traditional Santorini dishes like fava, tomatokeftedes, and grilled octopus, and don't be afraid to travel off the beaten road to find hidden gems. Finally, remember to savor your meals while admiring Santorini's gorgeous surroundings and distinct atmosphere.

Chapter 23: Santorini Wines and Wine Regions

Assyrtiko Dry White Wine
The vines are grown in low basket-shaped crowns close to the ground to protect them from high winds.

The nocturnal fog, which comes off the sea, gives much needed water to the vines during the scorching summer nights and, along with the invigorating northerly winds, creates great growing conditions for the formation of the superb Santorini wines.

Santorini white wines are extraordinarily dry, with a characteristic citrus bouquet and traces of smoke and minerals from the volcanic soil.

The dessert wines of Santorini are known as 'Vinsanto,' a derivative of the island's name.

Vinsanto can be naturally sweet or fortified, and it must be matured in barrels for at least two years.

It stands out for its wonderful silky palate and scents of creme brulee, chocolate, and dried apricots.

Nykteri Dry White Wine

Superior quality Santorini Appellation of Origin. Since 3,500 years, the Nykteri has been associated with Santorini's famous white wines.

The technique for 'immediate wine making' on the same night that the grapes were harvested solved the problem of the sensitive scent depreciation of the variety.

The Nykteri is a cross between the Assyrtico, Athiri, and Aidani types.

To preserve even the most delicate smells of fermentation, the winemaking temperature is kept below 18oC.

The wine is aged in barrels for at least three months. The wine's interaction with the barrel's wood imparts a unique delicacy to the Nykteri.

Characteristics

Wine that is crystal clear and semi-yellow. Aromas of jasmine, citrus fruits, florals, and pear dominate, and are accentuated by a subtle vanilla note.

A powerful body with a pleasant personality and a lingering aftertaste. It's served at 11-12°C.

It goes nicely with grilled meats and poultry, as well as traditional Greek recipes like tomato meatballs and fava dip.

Vinsanto: Santorini's Traditional Wine

Vinsanto is a renowned type of white wine originating from Santorini, known for its exceptional quality and sweet nature. Lois Lacroix, a notable 19th-century traveler, describes Vinsanto in his 1853 book "Ils de la Grece":

"There is no dessert wine that can compete with the white Santorini Vinsanto. It is made from grapes that are placed on the home terraces and exposed to the sun for 15 days before being pressed. After a year, it transforms into an excellent sweet wine..."

Production:

Vinsanto is produced traditionally, following the same time-honored process of sun-drying grapes. This method, unchanged over the years, involves the use of indigenous yeast without adding extra alcohol. The wine is often aged in barrels for an extended period before bottling.

Composition:

Originally believed to be a blend of white Asyrtiko and crimson Mandilaria grapes, the Santorini appellation now confirms that Vinsanto is made exclusively from Asyrtiko and Aidani grapes.

Characteristics:

Color: Orange-yellow with an intense brown gloss.

Aroma: Dominated by aging, spices, honey, raisins, and lemon flower.

Taste: Sweetness balanced by variety acidity, offering a rich, velvety texture with hints of honey and lemon.

Serving: Vinsanto is served chilled at temperatures between 6 to 8 degrees Celsius, making it an ideal dessert wine to enjoy alone or paired with fruits and sweets.

Vinsanto Vin De Liquer: Superior Quality Sun-Dried Grape Wine

Production:

Vinsanto Vin De Liquer is made using the traditional method of sun-drying grapes, specifically Assyrtiko and Aidani grapes, known for their maturity. The process involves meticulous monitoring of the fermentation process over several days.

Characteristics:

Color: Orange-red with a chestnut sheen.

Aroma: Aromatic spices like clove and cinnamon with notes of peach and dried fruits.

Taste: Balanced sweetness with alcohol and acidity, dominated by honey flavors.

Serving: Best served chilled at 9°C, it pairs well with sweets, ice cream, nuts, cheese, and foie gras dishes.

Wine Variations:

Wine for Mezzo:

Less sweetened Vinsanto typically made from a blend of sun-dried and un-raisined grapes.

High acidity with peach flavors and a lingering wildflower honey aftertaste, aged in oak for one year.

Brousko:

Originating from the Venetian era, it's a traditional dry red, white, or rose wine with local grape combinations.

Traditionally prepared through foot-pressing, fermentation on skins and stems, and barrel-aging.

Although the original style of traditional Brousko has evolved, remnants of its raw form can still be found on the island.

Chapter 24: Festivals and Cultural Celebrations in Santorini

Santorini is said to have more churches than residences and more wine than water.

Because of their respect for tradition and faith, Santorinians tend to host religious feasts with gusto. Typically, preparations begin several days before the feast day. Cooking and religious decoration are among them. Every village celebrates its patron saint with distinct festivals and church services. The rite is extremely moving on Easter and the feast day of the Holy Virgin; villagers light candles and a procession circles Santorini's communities.

The following are details regarding cultural events and festivals in Santorini:

Cultural activities

Santorini hosts exciting cultural activities during the summer season. The following are the most important festivals:

• Festival Ifestia

Every August, Santorini hosts the Ifestia Festival (also known as the Greek Volcano Festival). It includes a fireworks display depicting the volcano eruption as well as a number of exciting events, concerts, and dance acts.

• Festival International de Musique

The International Music Festival brings international musicians to Fira for two weeks in September to perform.

• Easter In Santorini, Easter is observed with solemn splendor. On Holy Friday, the ambiance in the village of Pyrgos is particularly compelling, with candlelight diffused throughout the streets.

• May 29th

Akrotiri village celebrates Agia Theodosia's feast day.

• The feast day of Agioi Anargyroi is observed in Megalochori village on July 1st.

• The 20th of July

The feast day of Prophet Ilias is observed in the villages of Fira and Imerovigli.

• The 25th of July

Vothonos village celebrates Agia Anni's feast day.

• The 27th of July

Vourvoulos village celebrates Agios Panteleimon's feast day.

• 4th of August

Finikia village celebrates the feast of the Holy Seven Children.

• The 6th of August

The Transfiguration of Christ is commemorated in the communities of Pyrgos, Akrotiri, and Fira.

• The 15th of August

The feast day of the Diocese of the Virgin Mary is observed in Akrotiri, Firostefani, and the majority of Santorini's villages. The church of Panagia Episkopi hosts the largest festival in Santorini for the feast day of the Holy Virgin. The preparations begin the day before, with traditional food and local wine handed to the attendees.

• The 29th of August

Monolithos village celebrates Agios Ioannis' feast day.

• The 31st of August

Kamari village celebrates Agia Zoni's feast day.

• The 14th of September

The Holy Cross feast day is observed at Perissa village, at the Holy Cross church.

• The 20th of September

Kontohori village celebrates Agios Efstathios' feast day.

• The 24th of September

Kamari village celebrates Mary Myrtidiotissa's feast day.

• The 20th of October

The feast day of Agios Gerasimos is held at Firostefani village on October 20th.

• Tuesday, October 22nd

Emporio village celebrates the feast day of Agios Averkios, the patron of wine.

• The 26th of October

Messaria village celebrates Agios Dimitrios' feast day.

• The feast day of Agioi Anargyroi is observed at Messaria village on November 1st.

- The 11th of November

The feast day of Agios Minas is held in the church of Agios Minas in Fira village.

- The 6th of December

The feast day of Agios Nikolaos is observed in the Agios Nikolaos Monastery in Thira village.

- The 9th of December

Vothonos village celebrates Agia Anni's feast day.

- The 12th of December

Agios Spyridon's feast day is observed in the communities of Pyrgos, Emporio, and Oia.

- The 13th of December

Vourvoulos village celebrates Agios Efstratios' feast day.

- The 15th of December

Kontohori village celebrates Agios Eleftherios' feast day.

Chapter 25: Ideal Times to Visit Santorini

The best months to visit Santorini are September to October and April to May, when the weather is mild and crowds are few. Santorini, like the rest of the Cyclades, sees the most visitors throughout the summer, so make your reservations months in advance if you plan to visit between June and August. Looking for a good deal? Try winter, when room rates typically fall. Keep in mind that the average high temperature this season is only in the 50s (not ideal for sunbathing), and the region receives a lot of rain. All of the rain, on the other hand, makes for a very floral (and warm) spring season. Crowds will also be minimal in the spring, though tourists will begin to flood the islands in May.

Weather in Santorini

Month	Average Temperature (°F)	Average Precipitation (in)
Jan	57	2.8
Feb	50	1.69
Mar	57	1.57
Apr	50	0.63
May	60	0.43
Jun	52	0
Jul	65	0.28
Aug	56	0
Sep	73	0.43
Oct	62	1.5
Nov	81	2.32

What You Need to Know

Take a sip
The rich volcanic soil of Santorini is great for cultivating grapes, therefore wine is the beverage of choice here. Try some of the greatest at a local taverna.

Do not walk barefoot on the beach.
Santorini's beaches are mostly constructed of tiny pebbles rather than sand, which makes them quite hot after a few hours in the sun. Wear sandals or water shoes to avoid getting burned.

Santorini isn't only about cliffs.
The photos of Santorini that show it high on the cliffs are really from the island's west shore. The east coast, which includes Kamari and Perissa, is mostly flat.

Saving Money in Santorini

Vacation during the off-seasons Warm weather is common in the fall and spring, but it is not as popular with tourists as it is in the summer. If you avoid the summer throngs, you can get some fantastic hotel deals.

Hungry? Go inland.

While the prospect of eating fresh Greek meals on the beach or cliffside is undoubtedly appealing, certain eateries may demand greater costs purely because of their location. Take advantage of these picturesque restaurants, but balance it out by going inland, where you'll most likely find more affordable menus.

Keep to the east shore.

Hotels along the caldera, such as the famed Oia, tend to attract the most visitors, particularly honeymooners. Rooms in southeastern towns like Kamari and Perissa are substantially more affordable.

Customs and Culture

The official language is Greek, although with the island's massive influx of visitors (as many as 10,000 cruise ship tourists arrive daily), you're more likely to encounter English-speaking Greeks than not, especially in tourist areas. Understanding body language is essential in this situation. Be mindful of your movements. For example, using your thumb and index finger to signify "OK" is inappropriate, as is holding your palm up to anyone. Make sure your hand is facing you if you wish to wave farewell. In terms of signifying 'yes' and 'no,' nodding your head to indicate 'yes' and shaking your head to indicate 'no.' The Greeks do things differently. A slight downward nod indicates 'yes,' while a slight upward nod indicates 'no.' These motions are frequently subtle and rapid, making them difficult for foreigners to grasp. To prevent getting lost in body language translation, avoid attempting to communicate with gestures here.

Greeks are well-known for their friendliness, especially when meeting new people. Shaking hands is common when greeting a Greek in a social setting. When meeting new people, it is customary to exchange two kisses, one on each cheek. When it comes to communication, Greeks are known to be quite open and deeply engaged. They have also been known to get very personal, very quickly. If you're uncomfortable with the conversation, such as discussing sensitive topics like politics or being asked too intimate questions, simply shift the subject. Lateness is very prevalent here. Expect Greeks to be at least 15 minutes late if you have plans with them.

Walking about the towns or beaches, some of which are dress optional, is permitted in shorts and T-shirts. Even in restaurants, dress is casual, but Greeks tend to dress up a little more nicely while dining out in the evenings. Except on the beach, never enter a restaurant or public venue in your bathing suit or barefoot, even if you're walking down a beachside promenade.

The euro is the currency of Santorini. Because the euro to US dollar exchange rate changes, make sure to check the current currency rate before you travel. Most restaurants and shops accept major credit cards. When dining out, a service charge may be included. As a result, tipping is uncommon. Also, keep in mind that the plumbing system in Santorini isn't great; instead of flushing old toilet paper down the toilet, place it in the waste basket to avoid potentially embarrassing flooding scenarios.

How to Eat

Take advantage of the wonderful Greek cuisine when visiting Santorini. The flavors of the fruits and vegetables cultivated on the island are enhanced by the island's temperature and volcanic soil. As a result, Santorini has earned a name for itself in the wine community, with a visit to one of the island's vineyards ranking among the island's top attractions. In addition to exquisite grapes, make sure to include cherry tomatoes (particularly sun-dried), capers, and white eggplant in one or more of your meals while in Santorini. The sweetness and white color of the eggplants cultivated here are directly related to the volcanic soil. Cherry tomatoes are another fruit whose flavor can be attributed to the soil. If you like eggplant, you'll love moussaka, a Greek-style lasagna with layers of eggplant, minced meat, fixings, and spices topped with béchamel sauce. Other must-try Greek dishes include anything containing olives and olive oil, particularly a traditional Greek salad, and fava, a traditional dip prepared from fava bean puree.

Greeks are obsessed with dips. Along with fava and the famed tzatziki sauce (yogurt, cucumber, and garlic), taramasalata, created from smoked fish roe and combined with olive oil and lemon juice, is a must-try and uber-traditional dip. Dolmades and keftedes are two other popular little snacks. Dolmades are seasoned rice that is often mixed with meat or vegetables and wrapped totally in a grape or vine leaf. Keftedes are fritters that are typically stuffed with cherry tomatoes (tomatokeftedes) or grated zucchini (kolokithokeftedes). If you're looking for something heartier, you're in luck: grilled meats are popular on the island, as well as throughout Greece. Souvlaki, or seasoned skewered meat, is commonly served with tzatziki. Octopus is very popular, and you may often find it hanging by its tentacles outside seaside tavernas. You can't leave without getting a gyro, of course. Make room for dessert, which includes baklava, a filo pastry covered with honey and crushed nuts, and loukoumades, or deep-fried donut holes coated with hot honey and cinnamon.

Santorini has everything from quick gyros to informal diners to expensive restaurants. Fine dining and expertly prepared Mediterranean cuisine can be found at Restaurant 1800 in Oia. If possible, reserve a table on the roof to enjoy panoramic views of the island's cliffs. Another expensive choice is Selene, which is conveniently located in Pyrgros, which is home to several wineries. Taverna Nikolas in Fira is as traditional as it gets, serving classic Greek cuisine at reasonable pricing. Enjoy a candle-lit dinner at Ambrosia on the caldera's edge for a touch of romanticism.

Safety

Santorini is relatively safe. Travelers report feeling safe going around the streets both during the day and at night. Pickpocketing is also rare in this area. There aren't many sidewalks in Santorini, so be cautious when walking the streets as you may need to dodge the occasional rogue, rapid scooter. Use caution when exploring Santorini's beaches. Most, if not all, of the beaches are made up of small rocks rather than sand and, in the summer, can become too hot to touch with bare feet. Bring beach sandals or water shoes to protect yourself from sunburn. The tap water in this area is unsafe to drink.

How to Get Around Santorini

Walking or taking the bus are the best ways to get around Santorini. It's easy to walk around the tiny seaside communities, but the bus is the easiest way to travel from one to the other. KTEL bus services connect Fira (the capital city) to a variety of sites on the main island. Although KTEL serves the Santorini (Thira) Island National Airport (JTR), you may find it quicker to take a taxi into town. If you want to do some island hopping, take a ferry from Athinios (approximately 5 miles south of Fira).

Requirements for Entry and Exit

To enter Greece, you must have a passport that is valid for the duration of your visit and for at least six months thereafter. A visa is not required unless you want to remain for more than 90 days. More information on entry and exit requirements can be found on the website of the United States State Department.

The Oia district is commonly seen in images of Santorini. The neighborhood is densely packed with white and pastel-colored structures that cascade down cliffsides. Staying here will cost you a hefty fortune, given its popularity and plenty of luxurious hotels.

Printed in Great Britain
by Amazon